The Psyche in Antiquity

BOOK ONE

Early Greek Philosophy

— From Thales to Plotinus —

EDWARD F. EDINGER

Edited by Deborah A. Wesley

See final page for other titles in this series by Edward F. Edinger

Canadian Cataloguing in Publication Data

Edinger, Edward F. (Edward Ferdinand), 1922-1998
   The psyche in antiquity

(Studies in Jungian psychology by Jungian analysts; 85-86)

Contents:
bk. 1. Early Greek philosophy
bk. 2. Gnosticism and early Christianity

Includes bibliographical references and index.

ISBN 0-919123-86-4 (v. 1)
ISBN 0-919123-87-2 (v. 2)

1. Jungian psychology.
2. Philosophy, Ancient—Psychological aspects
3. Jung, C.G. (Carl Gustav), 1875-1961.
I. Wesley, Deborah A. II. Title. III. Series.

BF175.4.P45E34 1999   150.19'54   C99-930320-1

INNER CITY BOOKS
Box 1271, Station Q, Toronto, Canada M4T 2P4

Telephone (416) 927-0355 / FAX (416) 924-1814
Web site: www.inforamp.net/~icb / E-mail: icb@inforamp.net

Honorary Patron: Marie-Louise von Franz.
Publisher and General Editor: Daryl Sharp.
Senior Editor: V. Cowan.

INNER CITY BOOKS was founded in 1980 to promote the
understanding and practical application of the work of C.G. Jung.

Cover: Lino prints by Vicki Cowan, © 1999.

Printed and bound in Canada by University of Toronto Press Incorporated

Contents

Author's Note

The Psyche in Antiquity began as two lecture series given at the C.G. Jung Institute in Los Angeles in the winters of 1993 and 1994. Book One *(Early Greek Philosophy)* and Book Two *(Gnosticism and Early Christianity)* were originally transcribed from audiotape by Charles Yates, M.D., who also, along with Dianne Cordic, partially edited Book One. Deborah Wesley edited Book Two, completed work on Book One, and unified the style of the whole. The illustrations are by Charlene M. Sieg.

I thank all for their devoted work and especially Deborah Wesley for bearing the responsibility for putting this difficult material into final form.

Edward F. Edinger
Los Angeles

Illustrations

1
Introduction

Depth psychotherapy and nuclear physics are unique phenomena of the twenti-
eth century, and in certain respects have no predecessors. Because of this, a little
explanation is needed as to why this book arising from depth psychotherapy, a
most modern vocation, should take up material from so long ago. Although
depth psychotherapy is original, born almost *sui generis,* in its practical application it is the heir of three noble traditions: the medical tradition of the care of
patients, the religious tradition of concern for the soul, and the philosophical
tradition of dialogue in the search for truth. This particular study centers on the
third tradition, the philosophical one.

The early Greek philosophers were the first to articulate certain ideas and
images that are central to the Western psyche. It behooves depth psychologists
to be familiar with these images and their origins and to recognize them as they
appear in modern dreams and other psychic contents. We know that many cul-
tures hold it vital to their well-being to be in touch with their ancestors; it promotes our psychological health as well to be in touch with the early Greeks, our
cultural ancestors. Such study connects us with our own psychic roots, which
reside in the collective unconscious, laid down like geological strata during the
evolution of the human psyche.

In general the human embryo's physical development echoes the stages of
the evolution of the species, a parallel expressed as "ontogeny recapitulates
phylogeny." Something of the same sort happens in psychological development.
As a personal analysis leads one back to childhood or family origins, it returns
one at the same time not just to personal childhood but also to the childhood of
the species. Knowledge of these earlier ideas and psychic images as they were
experienced by the human race as a whole is relevant for the analyst at a practical level.

C. G. Jung speaks of this:

In consequence of the collective nature of the [archetypal] image it is often impossible to establish its full range of meaning from the associative material of a single
individual. But since it is of importance to do this for practical therapeutic purposes, the necessity of comparative research into symbols for medical psychology
becomes evident on these grounds also. For this purpose the investigator must turn
back to those periods in human history when symbol formation still went on unim-

7

peded, that is, when there was still no epistemological criticism of the formation of images.[1]

This certainly applies to the early Greeks. They had no epistemological criticism of the metaphysical doctrines they spun out and projected onto the universe. What they espoused was almost pure psychology. It was the phenomenology of the psyche expressing itself in a naive way.

In a later work, Jung states:

> Any renewal not deeply rooted in the best spiritual tradition is ephemeral; but the dominant that grows from historical roots acts like a living being within the ego-bound man. He does not possess it, it possesses him.[2]

That remark speaks to the practical importance of making these archetypal amplifications in the course of the analytic process. The psychological renewal that the patient experiences in analysis becomes rooted in the best spiritual tradition of the human race and not just in the shallow roots of his or her own personal life. Certainly ancient Greek philosophy is part of our best spiritual tradition. If we are not connected to these roots, we are ephemeral.

The early Greeks stood at the dawn of rational human consciousness. They had just stepped out of the mists of *participation mystique* with nature. They were beginning to reflect on the nature of human existence with a bit of objectivity. Wordsworth characterizes this transition in "Ode: On Intimations of Immortality from Recollections of Early Childhood":

> There was a time when meadow, grove, and stream,
> The earth, and every common sight,
>   To me did seem
> Apparell'd in celestial light,
> The glory and the freshness of a dream.
> It is not now as it hath been of yore; . . .
>
> Our birth is but a sleep and a forgetting:
> The Soul that rises with us, our life's Star,
>   Hath had elsewhere its setting,
>   And cometh from afar:
>   Not in entire forgetfulness,
>   And not in utter nakedness,
> But trailing clouds of glory do we come
>   From God, who is our home:

---

[1] "The Philosophical Tree," *Alchemical Studies,* CW 13, par. 353. [CW refers throughout to *The Collected Works of C.G. Jung]*
[2] *Mysterium Coniunctionis,* CW 14, par. 521.

Heaven lies about us in our infancy![3]

We can think of the early Greek philosophers similarly: they are trailing clouds of glory, so to speak. They are not abstract rationalists; they are just stepping out of identification with the archetypal psyche, trailing clouds of that dimension with them. This means that their concepts and images are laden with the numinosity that accompanies all newborn things. When these same ideas are paralleled in the dreams and fantasies of patients in analysis, recognizing such connections is highly therapeutic.

The modern notion of a philosopher is that of an academic, dry-as-dust rationalist. The early tradition of philosophy was anything but that. Philosophers were visionaries, quite similar to the great Hebrew prophets. Like the prophets they were gripped by the numinosity of certain archetypal images. The prophets proclaimed the reality of their visions in the idiom to which they were born: the Hebrew religion. Similarly the Greek philosophers expressed their visions in their particular idiom, the language of dawning Greek rationalism. They were attempting to conceptualize the images that gripped them. It is no coincidence that Thales, the first documented Greek philosopher, became prominent in 585 B.C., the year of the capture of Jerusalem by Babylon and the deportation of the Israelites, their exile and the prophetic activity of Jeremiah and Ezekiel.

It is my premise that philosophy, especially early philosophy, like religion, is primarily psychology. It is the phenomenology of the psyche revealing itself in a particular setting, rather than an abstract intellectual discourse. Nietzsche was perhaps the first person to recognize this. In *Beyond Good and Evil,* he says:

> Gradually it has become clear to me what every great philosophy so far has been: namely, the personal confession of its author and a kind of involuntary and unconscious memoir.[4]

Jung agrees that the psyche is the foundation of all philosophical assertions:

> How much "soul" is projected into the unknown in the world of external appearances is, of course, familiar to anyone acquainted with the natural science and natural philosophy of the ancients. It is, in fact, so much that we are absolutely incapable of saying how the world is constituted in itself—and always shall be, since we are obliged to convert physical events into psychic processes as soon as we want to say anything about knowledge.[5]

---

[3] *Poetical Works,* p. 460.

[4] Sect. 6, p. 13.

[5] *The Archetypes and the Collective Unconscious,* CW 9i, par. 116.

It does not surprise me that psychology debouches into philosophy, for the thinking that underlies philosophy is after all a psychic activity which, as such, is the proper study of psychology. I always think of psychology as encompassing the whole of the psyche, and that includes philosophy and theology and many other things besides. For underlying all philosophies and all religions are the facts of the human soul, which may ultimately be the arbiters of truth and error.[6]

Looking over the phenomenon of Greek philosophy as a whole, one has the impression that the initial and overriding interest of the Greek philosophers was in what lies beyond the visible world. They sensed that there was something behind what was ordinarily seen. Their basic questions were metaphysical, that is, beyond the physical. It is remarkable to see that the dawning rational consciousness of our species made that assumption so gratuitously: that there is something beyond what one can see. As we now understand it, that assumption demonstrates the projection of the reality of the psyche, which lies behind sensible, concrete existence.

John Burnet, who was a scholar of Greek philosophy in the earlier part of the century, grasped this same idea. He does not refer to the psyche per se but he makes the same point. Burnet speaks as a classicist:

Greek philosophy . . . is dominated from beginning to end by the problem of reality [meaning metaphysical reality]. In the last resort the question is always: "What is real?". . .

The problem of reality, in fact, involves the problem of man's relation to it, which at once takes us beyond pure science. We have to ask whether the mind of man can have any contact with reality at all, and if it can, what difference this will make to his life. To anyone who has tried to live in sympathy with the Greek philosophers, the suggestion that they were "intellectualists" must seem ludicrous. On the contrary, Greek philosophy is based on the faith that reality is divine, and that the one thing needful is for the soul, which is akin to the divine, to enter into communion with it. It was in truth an effort to satisfy what we call the religious instinct. Ancient religion was a somewhat external thing, and made little appeal to this except in the "mysteries," and even the mysteries were apt to become external, and were peculiarly liable to corruption. We shall see again and again that philosophy sought to do for men what the mysteries could only do in part, and that it therefore includes most of what we should now call religion.[7]

It is interesting to observe how this problem of the nature of reality had evolved by the time of Plato, about 200 years after Thales. By then the issue had

---

[6] "General Aspects of Dream Psychology," *The Structure and Dynamics of the Psyche,* CW 8, par. 525.
[7] *Greek Philosophy: Thales to Plato,* pp. 11f.

polarized into two opposing views, which Plato describes in "The Sophist" in terms of a battle between gods and giants. One must recall that in early Greek mythology the Olympian gods destroyed the Titans in a great war. The Olympian deities then became the rulers. Plato refers to this as he says:

> What we shall see is something like a battle of gods and giants going on between them over their quarrel about reality.
>
> . . . One party is trying to drag everything down to earth out of heaven and the unseen, literally grasping rocks and trees in their hands, for they lay hold of every stock and stone and strenuously affirm that real existence belongs only to that which can be handled and offers resistance to the touch. They define reality as the same thing as body, and as soon as one of the opposite party asserts that anything without a body is real, they are utterly contemptuous and will not listen . . . .
>
> [The listener in the dialogue responds:] The people you describe are certainly a formidable crew. I have met quite a number of them before now.
>
> [The speaker continues:] . . . Yes, and accordingly their adversaries are very wary in defending their position somewhere in the heights of the unseen, maintaining with all their force that true reality consists in certain intelligible and bodiless forms. In the clash of argument they shatter and pulverize those bodies which their opponents wield, and what those others allege to be true reality they call, not real being but a sort of moving process of becoming. On this issue an interminable battle is always going on between the two camps.[8]

The battle between the gods and giants, which began over two thousand years ago, is not over yet.

Greek philosophy has its own particular psychological context in antiquity. It was only one of a number of currents which came together as the sources of the modern Western psyche. The figure on the next page shows some of these currents. Each will be described in turn to show how Greek philosophy fits into the larger context of antiquity. One can think of them as rivers which join each other when the conditions are right.

The Hebrew source is one of the largest, chiefly through the Old Testament. A Babylonian tributary has poured itself into that great Hebrew river, so that if you look closely at the Hebrew Bible you will find Babylonian mythology there also. A small stream from the Hebrew river joins a small one from the Greek river, ending in Philo. He was the first to document explicitly the synthesis of Hebrew religion and Greek philosophy. Hebrew and Greek streams underwent another synthesis at a later time as the Jewish heresy, Christianity, joined Greek philosophy to create Christian theology. Another prominent stream is Persian

---

[8] Sect. 246a, in Edith Hamilton and Huntington Cairns, eds., *Plato's Collected Dialogues.*

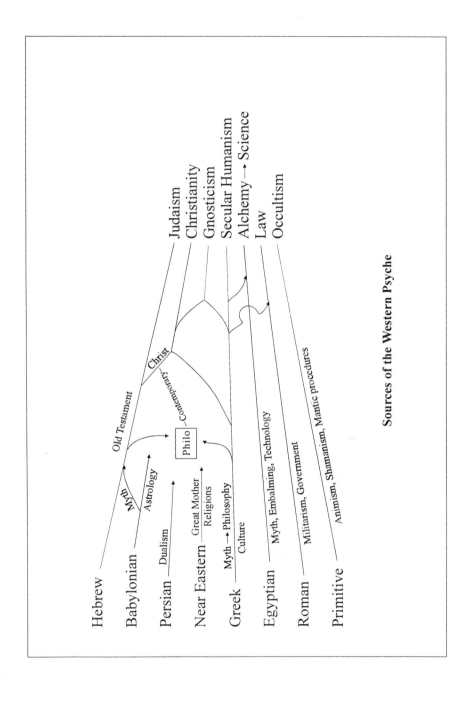

Sources of the Western Psyche

dualism, Zoroastrianism, later an aspect of Gnosticism also. The Near-Eastern Great Mother religions made real contributions to Christian theology as well, with the increasing emphasis on the Virgin Mary.

The other major river is the Greek one, which starts as mythology and develops into philosophy and culture in general, especially into the arts. The Hebrew and the Greek streams are the primary ones, which is signified in the traditional educational maxim that modern Western civilization is a product of Athens and Jerusalem. An important intermingling between the Greek and the Egyptian generated alchemy. The parents of alchemy are Egyptian embalming and technology, a practical tradition, and Greek philosophy. Alchemy later led into science itself, including depth psychology.

The Roman tradition was substantially influenced by the Greek. It appears largely in the realm of practical military and civic affairs and in the whole legacy of law. Finally there is the primitive stream, which is behind all the others and includes animism, shamanism and mantic procedures of various kinds, and which continued to live mixed into these other currents and is still alive today. Greek philosophy is in a central position, having interacted with almost all the other streams in its vicinity.

This book is organized around fourteen major personalities in the history of Greek philosophy. Jung, who refers to all of them in his *Collected Works,* has included the main Greek tradition in the body of data he used in his formulation of the psyche. Each of these fourteen is associated with one or more central concepts or metaphysical images. Nietzsche observed that the Greeks have embodied for us "all the eternal types [and] . . . all the archetypes of philosophical thought."[9] These archetypal ideas which gripped the Greek philosophers have given birth to and underlie much human reflection.

For the early Greeks, philosophy was a way to study the archetypes. The word *philosophia* in Greek means "love of Sophia," and philosopher means "lover of Sophia," that is, of Wisdom. In some settings Sophia was highly personified. In the Hebrew wisdom literature and in Gnosticism, Sophia was the feminine consort of the Deity. At the root of the word *philosophia* is the image of a love affair with a goddess. F.E. Peters, in his lexicon of Greek terms, says:

> By the traditional Greek account Pythagoras was the first to use the term *philosophia* and endowed the word with a strongly religious and ethical sense . . . which can best be seen in the view of the philosopher put forth by Socrates in *Phaedo*

---

[9] *Philosophy in the Tragic Age of the Greeks*, p. 2.

62c-69e. In Aristotle it has lost these Pythagorean overtones . . . *philosophia* has now become a synonym for *episteme,* in the sense of an intellectual discipline seeking out causes.[10]

The purpose of this book, however, is not to study philosophy, but to track the psyche as it manifests itself in early philosophy. The archetypal ideas which so gripped the early Greek philosophers are living psychic organisms and they undergo differentiation and evolution as various minds grapple with them. Eventually they become dried up, desiccated, so that what is left in Greek philosophy is an abstract skeleton, all structure and no life. In depth psychology, however, we still encounter these ideas as living organisms in the unconscious. Jungian psychology redeems the relevance of ancient philosophy.

Connecting one's individual experience of the psyche, its evolution and development, to the larger process of the evolution and development of the collective psyche as a whole, is of practical importance for the understanding of unconscious processes. If one accepts this premise, then only with the knowledge of these earlier expressions can the parallels with modern ones be seen. Then it is apparent that they manifest the same basic archetypal images.

Analysis attempts to bring about a renewal of the individual's psychology. It follows then that the most profound and the most satisfying and enduring renewal in the analytic process needs to be deeply rooted in the best spiritual tradition that the individual is a part of.

In the course of analysis the ego changes its standpoint. It finds a broader context. The personal, the contemporary, relates to a the larger perspective—if large enough, the perspective of eternity. It does, however, make quite a difference whether this takes place consciously or unconsciously. There is a world of difference between being unconsciously contained in a particular tradition and being consciously related to it.

---

[10] *Greek Philosophical Terms,* p. 156.

2
The Milesian Philosophers

The three Milesian philosophers, all from the city of Miletus, are usually considered as a group. Thales lived from about 585 B.C.; Anaximander, a student of Thales, lived from about 560 B.C. and Anaximenes, a student of Anaximander, lived about 546 B.C. As a group they brought to birth two primordial concepts: *physis* and *arche.*

Physis (in Latin, *natura;* in English, nature) is a profoundly complex and ambiguous term with a number of references. First, it is used for the source, origin, descent and lineage of something. Secondly, it refers to the natural, original condition of something, to a state or character of an entity, to its nature. Thirdly, it can refer to the efficacious, generative power of the organic world, the power of growth. The word *physis* derives from the root of the Greek verb *pheo-* meaning "to grow," thus it has an organic quality. As early as Aristotle, *physis* and God are mentioned in the same breath, both having the power to create things. Finally, *physis* refers to the regular order of things, an innate organic unity as contrasted with human law or human contrivance. Democritus, for example, says that men's lives are determined by the twin forces of nature and law, "nature" referring to an original organic or divine derivation. Among the Stoics *physis* became a god of the universe. Marcus Aurelius, a late Roman Stoic, says, "O Nature *[physis],* from you comes everything, in you is everything, to you goes everything."[11] A dictum of Chrysippus, one of the early Stoics, was: "Live by following [keeping close to] nature *[physis].* "[12]

The Hebrews lacked the Greek conception of nature. They had no term corresponding to *physis.* This meant that when the Old Testament was translated into Greek, *physis* did not appear because it did not exist as a concept. Philo was the first to make use of the word consciously. To him *physis* is no longer the origin or the creative power that it was for the early Greeks. Instead it has become an agent of divine activity. The Hebrew mentality, which gives priority to the religious dimension, had taken over the original word and subordinated it to its own usage.

In Gnosticism there appears the image of Sophia falling into the embrace of

---

[11] *New International Dictionary of New Testament Theology,* vol. 2, p. 657.

[12] Ibid., p. 658.

physis. Sophia, a divine personification, falls into nature and then calls out to be rescued. In early Greek alchemy we have the well-known dictum: "Nature rejoices in nature, nature subdues nature, nature rules over nature."[13] This indicates that nature is split and is in conflict with itself at a certain level.

The classical feeling toward nature was totally reversed by Christianity which demonized nature, turning her into an enemy of the spirit.[14] This is an outstanding feature of collective Christian psychology. With the coming of the Renaissance this attitude was again reversed, and nature was again given respect and consideration. Science gave her further respect by studying her.

When we reach the Age of Enlightenment, nature has been deified. The first sentence of the American Declaration of Independence, which was substantially a product of the French Enlightenment, reads:

> When in the course of human events it becomes necessary for one people to dissolve the political bands which have connected them with another and to assume among the powers of the earth the separate and equal station to which the laws of nature and of nature's God entitle them.

This is a late manifestation of *physis* appearing in modern political doctrine; "the laws of nature and of nature's God" represents the highest authority to which Jefferson could appeal. Finally, to bring the matter up to the present, Jung has taken the step of identifying the unconscious psyche with nature:

> The products of the unconscious are pure nature. "If we take Nature for our guide, we shall never go astray," said the ancients. [This is an old Stoic dictum]. But nature is not, in herself, a guide, for she is not there for man's sake. Ships are not guided by the phenomenon of magnetism. We have to make the compass a guide and, in addition, allow for a specific correction, for the needle does not even point exactly to the north. So it is with the guiding function of the unconscious. It can be used as a source of symbols, but with the necessary conscious correction that has to be applied to every natural phenomenon in order to make it serve our purpose.[15]

Jung is reminding us that the ego is not a piece of nature. It is, in fact, *contra naturam* to a very large extent. To use nature as its guide, the ego has to be very careful because nature is not interested in mankind.

There are modern words which have *physis* as a root: physics, physical, physician, physiology, physiognomy and so on. *Physis* is still a living entity in our evolving language.

---

[13] *Mysterium Coniunctionis,* CW 14, par. 21, n. 152.

[14] See *Symbols of Transformation,* CW 5, pars. 105ff.

[15] "The Role of the Unconscious," *Civilization in Transition,* CW 10, par. 34.

It is noteworthy indeed that *physis* was the first concept to crystallize out of early Greek philosophy. Considered psychologically, the discovery of *physis*, nature, means that one has perceived the separation between subject and object, between the ego and its surrounding environment, nature. The most basic prerequisite for consciousness is thereby established. Once there is an awareness that subject and object are two different entities, then a dialogue becomes possible between the ego, the subject, and nature, the object. Science becomes possible. In the physical sciences the ego asks questions of nature. By the way the questions are formulated and the experiments are set up, one coerces nature into giving specific answers. This works somewhat differently for the depth psychologist, in that although one puts questions to nature, nature also puts questions to us. Each patient is a part of nature submitting a question for us to answer. What follows is a two-way dialogue, unlike pure physical science. In one case humanity is experimenting on nature, and in the other case nature is also experimenting on humanity.

The other fundamental concept of the Milesians is the term *arche*. It means beginning; principle; original substance; in German, *urstoff*, ruling element. In alchemy the term *arche* was translated as *prima materia* or first matter. Derivatives with the stem *arche-* include such words as archetype, archeology, archaic; then, monarchy, patriarchy, etc.—those terms refer to the "first" as the ruler; the *arche*, since it comes first, is the ruler. Other such words are archbishop, archangel and so on. Understood psychologically, these terms refer to the projection onto the material world of an elemental, original condition of the psyche.

In this projection, the psyche announces the fact that it derives from an original, prime matter, and the conceptual image *arche* expresses the nature of the primordial state of the unconscious. It is quite remarkable that early in Western speculation, the unity of the psychic Self should be projected into the world in spite of the latter's obvious multiplicity. The world obviously does not derive from one individual stuff; it is a multiplicity. The assumption that there is an original *arche* that lies behind the multiplicity is a daring one, yet it is made quite naively. No one argued about the basic assumption that there was one thing as an origin. Rather, they argued about the nature of the one thing.

Of the three Milesians, Thales is a semi-legendary character. Some of the remarks preserved about him have an almost mythical quality. Interestingly, the name Thales is close to the Greek word for sea, *thalassa*. Thales, who thought water was the *arche*, may have a name which is the Greek equivalent of "seaman." He announced that the *arche* was *hydor*, water. So one could say that the first Western philosopher believed that the unconscious psyche is equivalent to water. It is a familiar image, akin to the understanding of water symbolism in dreams. The alchemists certainly picked up this idea, applying alchemical procedures to the *arche*, the *prima materia,* saying that in the course of making the Philosophers' Stone one must first reduce the *materia* one was dealing with to its original *arche*—which many thought of as water—by means of a *solutio.* Various kinds of water were thought of as the end goal of the alchemical process: the *hydor theion* or divine water, the *aqua vita,* the *aqua permanens.*

The Gnostic Naasenes equated their serpent, Naas, with Thales' concept of water. It will become apparent that both alchemy and Gnosticism are products of the primitive conceptions of Greek philosophy. For example Jung says:

> The Naasenes themselves considered Naas, the serpent, to be their central deity, and they explained it as the "moist substance," in agreement with Thales of Miletus, who said water was the prime substance on which all life depended. Similarly, all living things depend on the Naas; "it contains within itself, like the horn of the one-horned bull, the beauty of all things." It "pervades everything, like the water that flows out of Edem and divides into four sources."[16]

The living vitality of the symbol was demonstrated as subsequent symbol systems picked up and amplified the original. A symbol has the power to draw various other images to it in an organic process of amplification. Thales even shows up in the nineteenth century in Goethe's *Faust,* Part Two. In the Aegean sea festival scene at the end of act two, Thales appears and leads the homunculus to the sea and to his experience of the epiphany of the sea goddess. Thales sings a paean to water:

> Hail, hail, once again. How I exult, possessed as I am with the true and the beautiful. . . . Everything came out of the water. Everything is sustained by the water. Ocean, may you hold your sway for ever. If you didn't send your clouds, and brooks in abundance, and streams twisting this way and that, and the great rivers, where would our mountains and plains be, where the world? It is you who keep life at its freshest.[17]

As can be seen, these early images and figures frequently appear in later examples of cultural history, an expression of the continuity of the collective psyche. One can perceive these symbols not just as dissociated layers or fragments but as living currents that run through the centuries.

---

[16] *Aion,* CW 9ii, par. 311.

[17] Act 2, lines 8432-8443, trans. Barker Fairley.

Anaximander, who flourished about 560 B.C., held that the *arche* was the *apeiron,* which means the boundless, the unlimited or the infinite. *Peiron* or *peiros* means limit. *A-* is a privative, so *apeiron* means unbounded. It announces the fact that the unconscious is fundamentally infinite or unlimited. Jung remarked, "The decisive question for man is: Is he related to something infinite or not?"[18] The German word used by Jung for infinite is *unendliches,* exactly Anaximander's word. Our experience of the unconscious, when we go deeply enough, leads to implications of this sort. The Self,[19] as we understand it in its phenomenology, is beyond the limits of the ego to define and therefore, for the purposes of the ego, it is unlimited or infinite. That is what wholeness is when it is experienced by the ego.

Anaximander gives us our first significant fragment of Western philosophy:

> Things perish into those things out of which they have their birth, according to that which is ordained; for they give reparation to one another and pay the penalty of their injustice according to the disposition of time.[20]

This fragment seems to have a numinous power to fascinate scholars and commentators. Cornford's *From Religion to Philosophy* is no more than an extended commentary on this text of Anaximander, which is presented at the beginning of the book and followed by a long dissertation on its meaning.

Cornford's exposition is not psychological; however his understanding is that the multiplicity of individual, differentiated things we see around us is born out of an original *apeiron,* an original unlimited stuff, through the intermediaries of the four elements. This means that the *apeiron* first gives birth to the four elements. Then the individual things arise from various mixtures of the four elements. (This view is disputed by some scholars, as the four elements had not yet been delineated as such.) The four elements in various mixtures bring to birth the multiple objects in the world and then, when these objects perish, they return to the four elements from which they came, as punishment for their injustice in coming into existence. Their existence was a crime for which a penalty or reparation must be paid.

It is probably more suitable to think of the multiplicity of things as reverting

---

[18] *Memories, Dreams, Reflections,* p. 325.

[19] The Self is Jung's term for the central archetype expressing the totality of the psyche as organized around a dynamic center. It is experienced as the objective, transpersonal center of identity and cannot be empirically distinguished from the image of God.

[20] F.M. Cornford, *From Religion to Philosophy.* p. 8.

to the original *apeiron* when they die, rather than to the four elements. It is against the *apeiron* that the crime has been committed. Either way one looks at it, the remarkable fact remains that an ethical issue, justice or injustice, is attributed to nature, to a physical reality. This indicates that the psyche is still not differentiated from nature. If we extract this fact about the psyche from the physical world where it has been projected by Anaximander, we can then reformulate his statement thus: the existence of the conscious ego—which is what the multiplicity of the world refers to psychologically—is based on a crime or an injustice which requires reparation. It is a familiar idea, found for example in the myth of Prometheus stealing fire for mankind or in the myth of the fall of Adam in the garden of Eden. Understood psychologically both have the same meaning: human consciousness derives from a crime and is fundamentally guilt-laden.[21] Later, Empedocles makes reference to a prenatal crime to explain the nature of life on earth. Jung expresses the same idea:

> The opposites are the ineradicable and indispensable preconditions of all psychic life, so much so that life itself is guilt. Even a life dedicated to God is still lived by an ego, which speaks of an ego and asserts an ego in God's despite, which does not instantly merge itself with God but reserves for itself a freedom and a will which it sets up outside God and against him.[22]

One can read Jung's passage as a psychological paraphrase of Anaximander's text which says that things that pass away return to that infinite stuff out of which they came and pay reparation for their injustice. Jung speaks of the infinite as God in relation to the ego, which must pay for the injustice committed in being born into separate, individual existence. It is a subtle psychological point, but Jung states it unequivocally.

Cornford's discussion, of course, takes a different direction, as his interpretation is based on a different set of categories. He focuses on the term *chreon*, destiny, which can be translated as "what must be." Noting that fate and right are linked together, he discusses at length the term *moira*, which means lot or portion determined by the gods. Here he is still in the realm of mythology. Psychologically speaking, every individual human psyche, as it emerges and establishes itself out of the original totality of the unconscious, the original *apeiron* or infinite, takes on a specific character and a shape that is unique to it.

---

[21] This is further explored in my *Ego and Archetype: Individuation and the Religious Function of the Psyche*, pp. 16ff.

[22] *Mysterium Coniunctionis,* CW 14, par. 206.

For example, one particular psychological function is given preference over others, so that the more neglected functions are treated unjustly, so to speak. The particular lot or function or *moira* that determines what character an individual psyche will have, must necessarily be lopsided. There is no such thing as total symmetry in an individual human ego, so that each one has its own particular injustices as well, so to speak, which came with it into existence. This is another way of understanding Anaximander's text.

Later philosophers, notably Plato, elaborated the concept of *dike,* meaning justice or right behavior. They extracted it from the physical world of Anaximander and put it in the context of ethics.

Finally there was the third Milesian, Anaximenes, who flourished about 546 B.C., and who announced that the first principle was *aer* (air). Peters's lexicon says about the concept of air:

> For Anaximenes the *apeiron* of Anaximander and the *arche* of all things was air, probably because of its connection with breath and life (cf. *pneuma*). It was, as were most of the pre-Socratic *archai,* divine. [It is important to realize that these early men thought of the original stuff as divine, *theion].* The later popularizer of *aer* was Diogenes of Apollonia who made it the substance of both soul *(psyche)* and mind *(nous).* . . . [A symbol which is alive "magnetically" attracts to it other things, so *psyche* and *nous* have also been associated with air.] The connection *aer*—pneuma—psyche—zoe [life]—*theion* [meaning divine] remained a constant one. The air-like nature of the soul is raised in [Plato's] *Phaedo.* . . . Since the heavenly bodies dwell in the *ether* [a kind of upper air], another possibility was that the soul might be absorbed into the stars. . . . This belief was incorporated into later Pythagoreanism, [which held that] . . . the *aer* between the moon and the earth was filled with *daimones* and heroes. [Later, in Philo, the *daimones* became angels.][23]

Peters here points out that, initially, Anaximenes stated that the original divine stuff was air. Later thinkers said that it is also soul or mind, and that the whole layer of air surrounding the earth—between the earth and the moon—is filled with spiritual, incorporeal beings. One finds this thinking even in Paul in the New Testament. It became widespread belief that air was the medium containing spiritual entities which affected human beings. The symbolism here is basically air-breath-wind-spirit. The later word *pneuma* became an image of immense importance for the thinkers who followed and for the psychology of modern dream interpretation, in which one encounters air, wind and tornadoes for example. The symbolism started with Anaximenes and a whole complex of

---

[23] *Greek Philosophical Terms*, p. 4.

symbolic images in which wind and spirit are equated.

To put it in a nutshell, this symbol combination refers to the invisible, autonomous dynamism of the objective psyche—the dynamic of the Self expressed in the symbolism of air and wind. Very likely the imagery derives from primitive observations of what was called the breath-soul. When a warrior died on the battlefield, he gave out a last breath, often associated with hallucinatory phenomena. We see it even today. Individuals witnessing a death will sometimes say that they see a wraith-like creature ascend from the mouth of the dying person. It is the old idea of the breath-soul which leaves the body at death to go back to its source, to the surrounding air.

3
Pythagoras

Pythagoras was born on Samos, an island just off the coast of Asia Minor at the eastern end of the Mediterranean. He lived about 530 B.C. As an adult he moved to Croton, on the southern shore of the Italian boot. The Pythagorean community developed there. Pythagoras is a semi-legendary figure—no first-hand writings by him remain. Furthermore, it is impossible to distinguish which documents come from him personally rather than from the Pythagorean brotherhood and school which surrounded and succeeded him. The personal figure overlaps with the collective that he founded. According to the surviving material, he had magical attributes, indicating that he was a shamanic figure. Pythagorean writings clearly show the transition from the primitive to the Hellenic streams of the ancient psyche.

A central concept of the Pythagoreans was *arithmos,* number. They were responsible for the discovery of numbers as a conceptual paradigm; they were gripped by the numinosity of numbers and experienced them as divine. The modern mind is so removed from this original experience that we take numbers for granted. If we are open enough to recapture our earliest childhood experiences, we can perhaps recall a similar feeling of fascination at the discovery of numbers. For example, one woman recalled that when as a girl she discovered Mendeleev's periodic table of the elements in chemistry, she had a religious experience. The periodic table is just a numerical arrangement of the elements; the elements are interrelated by their numbers. The Pythagoreans had a similar experience when they realized that numbers exist as separate entities that one can manipulate. For the Pythagoreans, number is the *arche*, the primordial stuff of the universe.

Number is a subject of considerable interest to the depth psychologist who frequently encounters number dreams, which are usually obscure and difficult to fathom. Jung's statements about numbers are a kind of psychological update of the Pythagoreans' discovery of them:

> There is something peculiar, one might even say mysterious, about numbers. They have never been entirely robbed of their numinous aura. . . . The sequence of natural numbers turns out to be unexpectedly more than a mere stringing together of identical units: it contains the whole of mathematics and everything yet to be discovered in this field. Number, therefore, is in one sense an unpredictable entity. . . .

Number helps more than anything else to bring order into the chaos of appearances. It is the predestined instrument for creating order, or for apprehending an already existing, but still unknown, regular arrangement or "orderedness." It may well be the most primitive element of order in the human mind. . . . Hence it is not such an audacious conclusion after all if we define number psychologically as an *archetype of order* which has become conscious. . . .

It is generally believed that numbers were *invented* or thought out by man, and are therefore nothing but concepts of quantities, containing nothing that was not previously put into them by the human intellect. But it is equally possible that numbers were *found* or discovered. In that case they are not only concepts but something more—autonomous entities which somehow contain more than just quantities. Unlike concepts, they are based not on any psychic conditions but on the quality of being themselves, on a "so-ness" that cannot be expressed by an intellectual concept.[24]

Now if we conceive numbers as having been *discovered,* and not merely *invented* as an instrument for counting, then on account of their mythological nature they belong to the realm of "godlike" human and animal figures and are just as archetypal as they. . . .

The role that numbers play in mythology and in the unconscious gives food for thought. They are an aspect of the physically real as well as of the psychically imaginary. They do not only count and measure, and are not merely quantitative; they also make qualitative statements and are therefore a mysterious something midway between myth and reality, partly discovered and partly invented. . . .

These hints are merely intended to point out to the reader that the opposition between the human world and the higher world is not absolute; the two are only relatively incommensurable, for the bridge between them is not entirely lacking. Between them stands the great mediator, Number, whose reality is valid in both worlds, as an archetype in its very essence.[25]

Those remarks are relevant when we encounter number dreams. Almost invariably such dreams will be of an archetypal nature pointing to what Jung calls the higher world, as distinguished from and beyond the human world, pointing to the trans-ego realm of the Self as contrasted with the personal, human world of ego-consciousness.[26] Jung speaks of the first ten numbers as representing "an abstract cosmogony derived from the monad."[27] The first ten numbers are the only basic ones, since in the decimal system the first ten keep repeating them-

---

[24] "Synchronicity: An Acausal Connecting Principle," *The Structure and Dynamics of the Psyche,* CW 8, pars. 870f.

[25] "Flying Saucers: A Modern Myth," *Civilization in Transition,* CW 10, pars. 776ff.

[26] For further discussion of this, see Marie-Louise von Franz, *Number and Time,* chap. 1.

[27] *Memories, Dreams, Reflections,* p. 311.

selves on higher and higher levels. There are basically nine numbers plus zero. As Jung says, that sequence symbolizes a whole cosmogony.

The Pythagoreans' fundamental conception of number was contained in what they called the *tetractys*, a triangular figure of the first four numbers made of points arranged as shown here. These four numbers add up to ten.

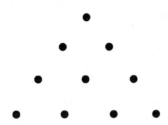

Walter Burkert, in his book on the Pythagoreans, says about the *tetractys*:

> The *tetractys*, a "tetrad" made up of unequal members, is a cryptic formula, only comprehensible to the initiated. . . . [It was spoken of as the answer to the question: What is the oracle of Delphi? The answer:] "The *tetractys*; that is, the harmony in which the Sirens sing." . . . The Sirens produce the music of the spheres, the whole universe is harmony and number, *arithmos*. . . . The *tetractys* has within it the secret of the world; and in this manner we can also understand the connection with Delphi, the seat of the highest and most secret wisdom.[28]

Somehow the secret of the world is to be found in number, especially as represented in the *tetractys*. The ancient Greeks did not have Arabic numerals available to them, so they used letters of the Greek alphabet as numbers or, more concretely, they used visual objects such as formations of pebbles to embody numbers.[29] The *tetractys* allows us to think of these first four numbers in visual or geometric terms.

The top of the triangle represents one point; geometrically it represents position without magnitude. Two points represent a line, since it takes two points to define a line; a line represents position plus a directional magni-tude, a one-dimensional entity. Three points define a plane; a plane represents position and direction plus breadth, a two-dimensional entity. Adding a fourth point to the plane produces a three-dimensional entity, a solid; a solid represents position, magnitude, breadth and depth.

---

[28] *Lore and Science in Ancient Pythagoreanism,* p. 187.

[29] Ibid., p. 72.

From the point of view of psychology, these early formulations are not only valid for the external world, but are also the projection of pure psychology. They represent the sequence of psychic development in infancy. Initially there is one point. Jung has demonstrated in *Mysterium Coniunctionis* how the point is a major symbol of the Self.[30] Nondimensional, it is a transcendent entity. It is the way the psyche begins, out of a "spark." The emergence of the second point corresponds to the beginning of a will, which includes the phenomenon of movement. The will moves directionally. Probably the first example of the movement of the will is the movement of the infant's eyes. The eyes lock in on an object indicating an interest in seeing, a directional movement. The addition of the third point, making a plane, corresponds to the formation of mental images, still of a two-dimensional nature as they have no concrete application. Finally with the emergence of the fourth point, to form a three-dimensional entity, there is a solidifying of all previous factors into a beginning ego, uniting the center, the willful movement and the imagery into a fourth capacity: the ability to engage the world around it. The engagement of the world in a meaningful way indicates a dawning ego-consciousness.

Analysis, of course, works in the reverse direction. In the course of analysis one starts with the fourth entity, the ego, and works backwards. Initially the patient is encountered in a personal, concrete, particular existence, in his fourfold structure. As we begin to use material from the unconscious including associations, we concentrate more on imagery separated from its concrete manifestation. As the process develops, the opposites are increasingly constellated until the conflict between the opposites is the major phenomenon. Finally, God willing, that state of opposition yields to a reconciling position in which the source, the monad, the Self, the single point, comes into view. This formulation can be seen as completely justifying the numinous quality that the Pythagoreans attached to the *tetractys.* It also corresponds to the Axiom of Maria, from alchemy: "One becomes two, two becomes three, and out of the third comes the one as the fourth."[31]

The three stages of the *coniunctio* can also be related to the stages of the *tetractys,* when the three stages are seen as the three transitions between the four phases of the *tetractys.* The three stages of the *coniunctio* are the following: 1) *unio mentalis*—the union of soul and spirit and their separation from the body;

---

[30] CW 14, pars. 36ff.

[31] See, for instance, *Psychology and Alchemy,* CW 12, par. 26.

2) this *unio mentalis* united with the body; 3) this second union of spirit, soul and body made one with the world, bringing about the *unus mundus.*[32]

Pythagoras is best known today for the Pythagorean theorem, taught in every high school geometry class. One can also reflect on this theorem from the point of view of psychology. Pythagoras is thought to have discovered that in a right triangle the square on the hypotenuse is equal to the sum of the squares on the other two sides. Although it is usual to think of this as $a^2 + b^2 = c^2$, the Pythagoreans thought of it quite concretely as square figures residing on those three sides, as shown in the figure on the next page.

This discovery was considered a divine disclosure. Pythagoras is said to have sacrificed an ox in gratitude for this revelation. The Pythagorean theorem is part of the discovery of irrational numbers, arising during the study of the diagonal of a square, a version of the Pythagorean theorem.

The figure on the next page also shows an example of a square with the side having a unit of 1. Applying the Pythagorean theorem, the diagonal of the square would then be the square root of 2, a result which was termed a *logos arithmos,* an irrational number. It is a number which cannot be precisely delineated: 1.4142136 . . . , with no conclusion. This was a disturbing fact for the ancients. It is parallel to the experience of an irrevocable encounter with the irrational, all the more shaking because it cannot be reconciled with rational constructs. The Pythagorean theorem, however, accomplishes a reconciliation in an interesting way: there is no solution until the problem is translated to a higher exponential level, that is, squared. Then reason is restored.

Similarly, in psychological terms, if problems on the concrete level of personal human existence are irreconcilable within the usual terms of understanding, then with the help of material from the unconscious such as dreams or fantasies—thus raising the problem to a symbolic level—the dilemma can often be resolved. This kind of solution is similar to the Pythagorean theorem which deals with the squares of the lines rather than the lines themselves. The lost *logos* is recovered at a higher level of abstraction.

Another Pythagorean concept is *enantia,* referring to the opposites. According to Aristotle, the Pythagoreans were the first to delineate the opposites, by establishing a table of ten pairs of them. Like numbers, the opposites carried numinosity. These original opposites were:

---

[32] See my *Mysterium Lectures: A Journey through Jung's* Mysterium Coniunctionis, pp. 277ff., for further discussion of the *tetractys* and the three stages of the *coniunctio.*

Pythagorean Theorem

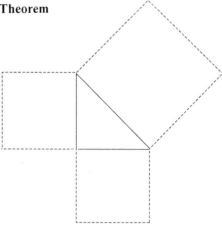

1. The square on the hypotenuse is equal to the sum of the squares on the other two sides.

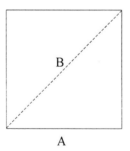

2. $A^2 + A^2 = B^2$. If $A = 1$, then $B = \sqrt{2}$ or $1.4142136\ldots$, an irrational number.

limit *(peras)*	unlimited *(apeiron)*
odd *(peritton)*	even *(artion)*
one *(hen)*	many *(plethos)*
right *(dexion)*	left *(aristeron)*
male *(arren)*	female *(thelu)*
resting *(eremoun)*	moving *(kinoumenon)*
straight *(euthu)*	curved *(kampulon)*
light *(phos)*	darkness *(skotos)*
good *(agathon)*	bad *(kakon)*
square *(tetragonon)*	oblong *(heteromekes)*

With the appearance of the opposites the world was rent asunder, and space was created for the growth of the human ego. The concrete image of the separation of the opposites is the ancient Egyptian cosmology of Geb and Nut, initially in a state of perpetual cohabitation, being pushed apart by their son until a bubble is created between sky and earth. Psychologically there is space for human consciousness to exist when the opposites are consciously separated and perceived as separate living entities.[33]

The Pythagoreans also maintained the idea of *palingenesia,* reincarnation. Pythagoras himself was supposed to have remembered many of his reincarnations. This is an idea that comes up in analysis occasionally. Perhaps a dream will hint at the idea that the dreamer had a previous life.

There is a striking example of this phenomenon in a case study published recently.[34] A woman, through dreams and impressions of waking consciousness, remembered her life in the thirteenth century in France as a Cathar, a heretic. She was able to recall accurately specific events and people from the past. This is a symbolic experience to take seriously but not naively. Very likely it is an experience of the collective unconscious. When a particularly intense experience is lived, it leaves a deposit in the collective unconscious which can be tapped into by later psyches. If one is living out of a particular archetype, one can become unconsciously identified with others who have lived out that same archetype. Although we do not have a full case history, this patient, a Catholic whom we are told was excommunicated, was perhaps by this experience put into a psychological condition analogous to the heretics of the thirteenth century. This could account for the unconscious identification with the Cathars, which then lived itself out in the symbolic imagery of reincarnation.

---

[33] For further discussion, see my *Anatomy of the Psyche: Alchemical Symbolism in Psychotherapy,* pp. 185ff.

[34] See Arthur Guirdham, *The Cathars and Reincarnation.*

The Pythagorean idea of reincarnation is the result of the influence of Orphism. The Orphics thought that life on earth was an expiation for crimes or impurities of previous lives. They were dedicated to the idea of *katharsis,* "purification" of their souls. They were vegetarian and highly ascetic, and concerned with how to escape the wheel of rebirth. A similar idea is seen in Empedocles. Plato, likewise, was influenced by Orphism in a more differentiated way. The *Phaedo* is an example of philosophic Orphism; Plato speaks of philosophic purification from pleasures and fears:

> Truth is in fact a purification from all these things, and self-restraint and justice and courage and wisdom itself are a kind of purification. And I fancy that those men who established the mysteries [Orphic mysteries] were not unenlightened, but in reality had a hidden meaning when they said long ago that whoever goes uninitiated and unsanctified to the other world will lie in the mire but he who arrives there initiated and purified will dwell with the gods. For as they say in the mysteries,"the thyrsus-bearers are many, but the mystics few;" and these mystics are, I believe, those who have been true philosophers. And I in my life have, so far as I could, left nothing undone, and have striven in every way to make myself one of them. But whether I have striven aright and have met with success, I believe I shall know clearly, when I have arrived there, very soon, if it is God's will.[35]

That is pure Orphism translated into philosophic terms. The initiated and purified ones are called the philosophers. In psychological terms those would be the ones who have submitted themselves to the rigors of the individuation process.[36] The mire that the uninitiated fall into represents the mud of the unconscious that has not been worked on psychologically, the *prima materia* which has not undergone any development.

The Pythagoreans also held to the notion of *koinonia*, fellowship. This derives from the word *koinos,* meaning "common." It is the stem of the term *koine,* which referred to the common language spoken around the beginning of the Christian era. The Pythagorean *koinonia*—fellowship, brotherhood, community—developed around its founder, reveals something about cult formation in general. It was a religious community whose discoveries were often kept secret, thought of as sacred. This illustrates how the experience of the numinosum in a common context can weld people together. Their collective experience becomes the container for the Self.

---

[35] 69B-D, in H.N. Fowler, trans., *Plato,* p. 241.

[36] Individuation is Jung's term for the conscious realization and fulfillment of one's unique being. It is associated with typical archetypal imagery and leads to the experiencing of the Self as the center of personality transcending the ego.

This is seen in some phenomena of the modern world, especially intense ethnic, religious and political collective identifications, which activate transpersonal libido and which can generate holy wars. *Koinonia* constellates as a natural phenomenon when the numinosum is experienced in a collective setting. Cornford comments on the Pythagorean collective:

> To this society men and women were admitted without distinction; they had all possessions in common, and a "common fellowship and mode of life." In particular, no individual member of the school was allowed to claim the credit of any discovery he might make. The significance of this rule has not been fully understood.[37]

An example of the rule comes out in the story of Hippasos of Metapontion, who published secret knowledge and

> was cast away at sea, as having committed an impiety and taken glory to himself for his discovery, whereas all discoveries belonged to "Him", for so they call Pythagoras. They say that a supernatural vengeance overtook those who published what belonged to Pythagoras. This supernatural or daemonic anger was the wrath of Pythagoras himself, who after his death remained what he had been in life—the daemon in whom all the life of his church was centered and incarnated. . . . What is to be gathered from the story of Hippasos is that the pious Pythagoreans believed the Master's spirit dwelt continually within his church, and was the source of all its inspiration. The impiety lay, not in divulging a discovery in mathematics, but in claiming to have invented what could only have come from "Him."[38]

There are, of course, examples of *koinonia* still existing today. It is a fundamental phenomenon of the psyche.

[handwritten margin note: Cite this for reference to the antiquity part.]

---

[37] *From Religion to Philosophy,* p. 202.
[38] Ibid., p. 203.

4
Heraclitus

Ephesus, on the coast of Asia Minor, was the site of the famous temple of Diana, for which the city was famous throughout the ancient world. Heraclitus was born there around 500 B.C. of a prominent aristocratic family, and there is reason to believe that members of his family were hereditary caretakers of the temple. Heraclitus' philosophy also was quite aristocratic. He was a kind of ancient H.L. Mencken. Mencken despised the ignorance and vulgarity of the masses, whom he referred to as "boobs of the Bible belt," and Heraclitus similarly ridiculed the religious practices of his time, such as the widespread use of animal sacrifice:

> They vainly purify themselves with blood when they are defiled: as though one were to step in the mud and try to wash it off with mud. Any man who saw him doing that would think he was mad. And they pray to these statues as though one were to gossip to the houses, not knowing who the gods and who the heroes are.[39]

Heraclitus was Jung's favorite ancient philosopher. There are about fifty references to him in the *Collected Works,* the letters and the seminars. The most striking of all is a passage in the letters, in which Jung speaks of Heraclitus as one of the ten pillars of the "bridge of the spirit which spans the morass of human history."[40] In another letter he writes:

> Time and again I have had the unfortunate experience—which also befell my illustrious predecessor Heraclitus—of being named "the Dark." Heraclitus probably understood this darkness as little as I do, but I have so often come up against this judgment that I have finally accustomed myself to thinking that either my views or my style must be so involved that they confront ordinary so-called sound commonsense with insoluble riddles.[41]

Several significant ideas have come down to us from Heraclitus. One is *pyr aeizoon.* The last part of the word, *-zoon,* derives from the same root as zoology or the woman's name, Zoe, which means life. *Pyr aeizoon* means ever-living

---

[39] Quoted in Jonathan Barnes, *Early Greek Philosophy*, p. 118.

[40] *Letters,* vol. 1, p. 89. (The other nine are: the Gilgamesh epic, the *I Ching*, the Upanishads, Lao-Tzu's *Tao-te-Ching*, the Gospel of St. John, the letters of St. Paul, Meister Eckhart, Dante and Goethe's *Faust*.)

[41] Ibid., p. 116.

fire, which for Heraclitus is the *arche.* He describes this fire as intelligence and the cause of the management of the universe. He expresses this by saying: "The thunderbolt steers all things."[42] By the thunderbolt, he means the eternal fire. In another passage, he says:

> The world, the same for all, neither any god nor any man made; but it was always and is and will be, fire ever-living, kindling in measures and being extinguished in measures . . . all things . . . are an exchange for fire and fire for all things, as goods are for gold and gold for goods.[43]

In other words, the other elements are derived from fire by various degrees of condensation. In this same context he spells out how the change of opposites occurs:

> [The change of opposites is] a path up and down, and the world is generated in accordance with it. For fire as it is condensed becomes moist, and as it coheres becomes water; water as it solidifies turns into earth—this is the path downwards.[44]

This passage refers to the path downward, which then reverses to become the path upward. In the path upward, the earth dissolves and becomes water, which then turns into vapor and thence into fire, which is at the basis of all the different degrees of aggregation.

According to this theory, energy is the basis of *physis,* which is quite a modern idea, and corresponds psychologically to the idea of libido, a concept that Jung developed very substantially in *Symbols of Transformation.*[45] There, libido is the central concept, and the forms it takes are seen as empty until energy is poured into them. In a certain sense, the libido theory of the psyche corresponds to the Heraclitean idea that fire is the fundamental *arche.*

Heraclitus connected the term *logos* with the concept of fire, although he did not develop the *logos* concept as explicitly as the later philosophers, primarily the Stoics. Certainly the later Stoics equated fire and *logos,* and they attributed the equation to Heraclitus.

Logos is a multifaceted term, especially in its early usage. Its basic meaning is "word," but it also meant "reason" and also an "account" or a "rational presentation based on reason," and hence, in addition, it had the implication of representing the rational principle in the universe. Heraclitus says:

---

[42] Quoted in Barnes, *Early Greek Philosophy,* p. 104.

[43] Ibid., pp. 122f.

[44] Ibid., p. 107.

[45] CW 5.

Of this account which holds forever men prove uncomprehending [What is translated as "account" here is the word *"logos,"* thus: Of this *logos,* which holds forever, men prove uncomprehending] both before hearing it and when first they have
heard it. For although all things come about in accordance with this account
[logos], they are like tiros as they try the words and the deeds which I expound as I
divide up each thing according to its nature and say how it is. Other men fail to
notice what they do when they are awake, just as they forget what they do when
asleep. . . .

For that reason, you must follow what is common *[koinos,* i.e., what is univer-
sal]. But although the account *[logos]* is common, most men live as though they
had an understanding of their own.[46]

What Heraclitus develops here is the fundamental issue that is always of concern psychologically: where does a given message or reaction or standpoint
come from? Does it come from the individual *logos* or does it come from the
universal *logos?* Does it come from the ego or does it come from the Self? That
is an ongoing question, both for oneself and for one's appraisal of the statements
of others.

Heraclitus was also well known for his doctrine of flux, *panta rhei,* which
means "all things flow"; everything is in a state of becoming; nothing is static
and fixed. These are not the exact words of Heraclitus, but this phrase has been
the summary formula of Heraclitus's doctrine since antiquity, so that tradition
has sanctified it. Heraclitus said:

On those who enter the same rivers, ever different waters flow. . . . We step and do
not step into the same rivers, we are and we are not. . . . For it is not possible to
step twice into the same river . . . nor to touch mortal substance twice in any condition: by the swiftness and speed of its change, it scatters and collects itself
again—or rather, it is not again and later but simultaneously that it comes together
and departs, approaches and retires.[47]

According to the historical accounts of Greek philosophy, the school of Heraclitus and the school of Elea, which was located on the western shore of Italy
and whose most famous representative was Parmenides, were in dispute over
this question of change. According to the Eleatics, Parmenides in particular, the
underlying nature of things is static: it does not move at all. According to Heraclitus, the exact opposite is true: everything flows. It is striking that so early in
Greek philosophy, a division on this metaphysical doctrine arises. One must
realize that neither philosopher is referring to concrete reality as experienced by

---

[46] Quoted in Barnes, *Early Greek Philosophy,* p. 101.

[47] Ibid., pp. 116f.

the senses. They are talking about the metaphysical reality that they think they can perceive behind the sensible world. In other words, in psychological terms, they are projecting psychological reality into the metaphysical dimension, and they reach opposite conclusions.

It is now possible to understand such a phenomenon, because we can see it as the conflict derived from the contrast between the ego and the Self. The ego is *panta rhei;* the ego flows constantly. One is not in the same mood from one hour to the next. One can wake up one way and go to bed in a totally different frame of mind: everything is *panta rhei* as far as the ego is concerned. But the Self, at least in the phenomenology that we observe in geometrical images, transcends time, and time is movement. Eternity is static; it is beyond the movement of time, so that as one is referring to the transpersonal center, the Self, the Eleatics would be right. When the two entities come together, when the Self starts to incarnate in a particular ego, it subjects itself to change and transformation, but it does not change on its own. It only changes when it encounters the moving, spatio-temporal dimensionality of egohood.

"Eternity" is a familiar translation of the term *aion.* This concept appears in one particular quotation from Heraclitus: "Eternity is a child at play, playing draughts: the kingdom is a child's."[48]

Jung used this quote, in different translation, on the stone that he carved and set up in his Bollingen retreat. In his memoirs, he translated the inscription as "Time is a child . . . ." The word is *aion* in Greek, and it is variously translated as "time," "eternity," or "an age," showing the ambiguity, the oppositeness that resides in the word. This helps to explain why Jung chose that quotation and also why he chose that particular term to be the title of his book, *Aion.* The word *aion* contains in itself simultaneously the idea of time, motion and becoming; and eternity, rest and being.

It is safe to assume that Jung took this passage in Heraclitus seriously, since he went to the trouble to carve it out laboriously on a piece of stone. The complete text of his inscription is:

Time is a child—playing like a child— playing a board game—the kingdom of the child. This is Telesphoros, who roams through the dark regions of this cosmos and glows like a star out of the depths. He points the way to the gates of the sun and to the land of dreams.[49]

---

[48] Ibid., p. 102.

[49] *Memories, Dreams, Reflections*, p. 227.

The first statement is taken out of Heraclitus, but other statements are mixed into the inscription. One can think of the text as a kind of highly condensed summary of Jungian psychology, lapidary in the true sense of the word.

Quite an important concept for the understanding of Heraclitus is the term *enantia,* which means "the opposites." For example:

War is father of all, king of all: some it shows as gods, some as men; some it makes slaves, some free.[50]

The path up and down is one and the same.[51]

Cold things grow hot, the hot cools, the wet dries, the parched moistens . . . beginning and end are common.[52]

Finally, there is quite an important fragment that Jung quotes: "Fate *[hymarmene]* is the logical product *[logos]* of enantiodromia, creator of all things."[53]

It is this insight concerning the opposites that so endears Heraclitus to Jung. John Burnet speaks about this particular insight as Heraclitus' fundamental thought:

Heraclitus looks down not only on the mass of men, but on all previous inquirers into nature. This must mean that he believed himself to have attained insight into some truth not hitherto recognized, though it was staring men in the face. To get at the central thing in his teaching, we must try then to find out what he was thinking of when he launched into those denunciations of human dullness and ignorance. The answer seems to be given in two fragments, 18 and 45. From them we gather that the truth hitherto ignored is that the many apparently independent and conflicting things we know are really one, and that, on the other hand, this one is also many. The "strife of opposites" is really an "attunement" *(harmonia).* From this it follows that wisdom is not a knowledge of many things, but the perception of the underlying unity of the warring opposites. That this really was the fundamental thought of Heraclitus is stated by Philo. He says: "For that which is made up of both the opposites is one; and, when the one is divided, the opposites are disclosed. Is not this just what the Greeks say their great and much belauded Herakleitos put in the forefront of his philosophy as summing it all up, and boasted of as a new discovery?"

Anaximander had taught that the opposites were separated out from the Boundless, but passed away into it once more, so paying the penalty to one another for their unjust encroachments. It is here implied that there is something wrong in

---

[50] Quoted in Barnes, *Early Greek Philosophy,* p. 102.

[51] Ibid., p. 103.

[52] Ibid., p. 115.

[53] *Psychological Types,* CW 6, par. 708, note 37.

the war of opposites, and that the existence of the opposites is a breach in the unity of the One. The truth Herakleitos proclaimed was that the world is at once one and many and that it is just the "opposite tension" of the opposites that constitutes the unity of the One.[54]

Burnet further refers to one of Heraclitus' fragments, in which he says: "Men do not know how what is at variance agrees with itself. It is an attunement of opposite tensions, like that of the bow and the lyre."[55]

That is the fundamental insight of Jungian psychology. A living, functional awareness of that fact, an operative knowledge of it that functions in one's daily life, not just abstractly, is indeed evidence of psychological wisdom. Such wisdom is not a knowledge of many facts but the perception of the underlying unity of the warring opposites.

Another major insight drew Jung to Heraclitus: an awareness of the Deity within the manifestations of the primordial psyche. Jung refers to this in an important passage in *Mysterium Coniunctionis,* which is a psychological commentary on an alchemical recipe. In discussing it, he touches on the theme of sulfur that requires cleansing. Sulfur is equated psychologically with desirousness. Jung paraphrases the alchemical recipe, saying:

Therefore away with your crude and vulgar desirousness, which childishly and shortsightedly sees only goals within its own narrow horizon. Admittedly sulfur is a vital spirit, a "Yetser Ha-ra," an evil spirit of passion, though like this an active element; useful as it is at times, it is an obstacle between you and your goal. The water of your interest is not pure, it is poisoned by the leprosy of desirousness which is the common ill. You too are infected with this collective sickness. Therefore bethink you for once . . . and consider: What is behind all this desirousness? A thirsting for the eternal, which as you see can never be satisfied with the best because it is "Hades" in whose honour the desirous "go mad and rave."[56]

The last sentence refers to a quotation from Heraclitus:

For if it were not to Dionysus that they made the procession and sung the hymn to the shameful [phallic] parts, the deed would be most shameless; but Hades and Dionysus, for whom they rave and celebrate Lenaean rites, are the same.[57]

What is so important about this passage from Heraclitus that it is mentioned

---

[54] *Early Greek Philosophy,* p. 143.

[55] Ibid., p. 136.

[56] CW 14, par. 192.

[57] Fragment 246, quoted in G.S. Kirk and J.E. Raven, *The Presocratic Philosophers,* p. 211.

in Jung's discussion of the alchemical recipe? Heraclitus has perceived and is expressing in this particular fragment that behind the lascivious passions celebrated by the phallic procession is the deity Dionysus. Hades is the infernal version of Dionysus, and it is as though the phallic hymns, when translated into their archetypal source, take on transpersonal numinosity. Jung inserts this particular reference to Heraclitus at just this point to illustrate that what he is stating is a piece of ancient wisdom that goes all the way back to Heraclitus.

What is behind all our desirousness? A thirsting for the eternal. But when we think we must have a particular object, whatever it is, when instinctual desirousness and lusts and greeds of all kinds are operating in concrete material terms, then Hades has taken over the role of Dionysus, because they are the same. This profound piece of wisdom is not to be understood on first hearing, and Jung links the insight with Heraclitus, which ennobles Heraclitus at the same time.

5
Parmenides and Anaxagoras

Parmenides

Although we know very little about Parmenides' personal life, he seems to have been an archaic wise man in the sense that he was both a philosopher and a notable lawgiver. He lived about 475 B.C. and came from Elea, on the southwestern coast of Italy, where a school of philosophy, the Eleatic school, was named after the city.

We have from Parmenides one short work, presented as a poem, which is divided into three parts. The "Prologue" gives a fanciful account of a heavenly trip in which Parmenides comes to the celestial domain of the goddess, who is to give him a revelation. We do not know whether this reflects some subjective experience or whether he was simply following an older poetic tradition. Either way, the theme shows that these early philosophers experienced their ideas as arising from divine revelation.

The next part is "The Way of Truth." The basic statement of this section is that "it is," and it is impossible to consider the idea that "it is not":

> Nor was it, nor will it be, since now it is all together, one, continuous. . . . That it came from what is not I shall not allow you to say or think—for it is not sayable or thinkable that it is not.[58]

Translated literally, the meaning of this passage is not entirely clear. However, when the word "reality" is substituted for the word "it," the meaning starts to become more apparent. The passage is saying that reality *is* and it cannot be considered that reality is *not*. The term "reality" can be replaced with the term, "the One," on the basis of Plato's dialogue, *Parmenides,* where "the One" is the chief subject of consideration. This is the same as saying that there is no such thing as nonexistence; the concept of nonbeing is inadmissible. Parmenides ends with a specific image of the *rotundum* in which he says that it, the One or this reality, is completed on all sides like the shape of a well-rounded ball, equal in every way from the middle, and therefore equal to itself on all sides.

The third part of Parmenides' poem is called "The Way of Opinions" or "The Way of Seeming" (in Greek, *doxa)* and concerns the nature of opinion versus the

---

[58] Quoted in Barnes, *Early Greek Philosophy,* p. 134.

nature of truth: "Here I cease for you my trustworthy argument and thought about the truth. Henceforward learn mortal opinions."[59]

Parmenides proceeds with a theory about the nature of *physis* (nature) and the universe, and what the heavens and the stars and the planets are made up of, the same as the other early physicists do. So here he shifts from the metaphysical world to the sensible world of visible appearances, and he says he includes this aspect, even though it is false and deceitful.

These two roads, the road of truth *(aletheia)* and the road of opinion *(doxa)* correspond to the archetypal level of the psyche and the personal level. At the archetypal level, duality does not exist. There are no opposites—there is only "the One." But as soon as a content reaches consciousness, it is split into two, a phenomenon of the operation of consciousness. Cosmogonic myths begin in the same way, with the split of the aboriginal unity into two. This way of truth, which is the road of *hen,* the One, corresponds to the original state of things before being split by ego-consciousness. The road of *doxa*—opinion, or seeming— is the way of duality or sensation. It is the way of ego experience.

An understanding of these terms—*aletheia* and *doxa*—that are basic to the roots of the Western psyche, deepens one's psychological insights. The Greek word for truth is *aletheia,* which is a privative, a negative term. It is a compound word: *a,* meaning "without," and *lethe,* referring to the water of forgetfulness which resides in the underworld. Lethe is a river which the deceased soul drinks from as it leaves earthly existence and enters Hades. As the soul drinks the water of Lethe, it forgets its previous life.

This also transpires at the other end of the cycle of birth and death, as demonstrated in Plato's "Myth of Er" at the conclusion of *The Republic.* Souls that are about to be born are required to drink the water of Lethe in order to forget their former heavenly existence when they enter this world in a new incarnation. This is an Orphic doctrine that was adopted by Plato.

It is remarkable that the word "truth" should be a privative, that what we consider to be a positive quality should be expressed by a negative term. A similar example of a privative that has a dynamic meaning for the modern mind is our word "unconscious." So *aletheia* or truth corresponds to our term "consciousness," and *lethe* would correspond to our term "unconsciousness." From the etymology we learn that in the Greek experience, the original principle is unconsciousness. *Lethe,* ignorance, is the original thing ("ignorance" is also a priva-

---

[59] Ibid., p. 136.

tive, meaning "not knowing"). From the standpoint of the modern psyche, however, the unconscious is a privative. We start out with the conscious ego, and as we work our way down, we reach a nonconscious state. The Greeks were so close to their psychic origins that they enshrined in their language the fact that the original state of the psyche is unconsciousness, which is a positive principle in itself.

The term *doxa* has some interesting features also, and over time has gone through a change of meaning. In early classical Greek, *doxa* meant "opinion," but it gradually evolved to mean "approval." In other words, if one has positive public opinion, then one is getting approval, which became "praise," and in more supreme form "glory." In New Testament Greek, the term *doxa* has become "glory." The theological term "doxology" refers to hymns of praise and glory to the Deity. The earlier meaning was "opinion," as something contrasted with truth and hence not highly thought of. These two terms *aletheia* and *doxa* would correspond to Plato's world of forms and ideas, on the one hand, which would be "truth," and to the world of sensible, visible material existence on the other hand— the world of opinion and of "seeming."

This question of true knowledge versus opinion is still a living one in psychology today, and brings up the whole question of psychological epistemology or the nature of knowledge. Psychology has a very shaky epistemological basis, because psychology, especially depth psychology, is an operation in which the psyche is passing judgment on itself. With the psyche, more than with any other subject matter, it is exceedingly difficult to distinguish between objective fact and personal bias. This is a serious problem if psychology is to claim a scientific status (although bodies of symbolism such as alchemy do provide us with an objective basis for understanding the psyche). It is possible to distinguish between psychic truth and psychic opinion, but the fact is that one experiences the psyche through one's individual subjectivity. There is no other way. This means that to establish true knowledge of the psyche, subjectivity must be objectified; that is the key phrase. Jung states this concept explicitly:

> Though I am sure of my subjective experience, I must impose on myself every conceivable restriction in interpreting it. I must guard against identifying with my subjective experience.[60]

One objectifies subjectivity by not identifying with it, or turning subjective experience into a universal truth (which almost everybody tends to do). One can

---

[60] *Letters,* vol. 2, p. 376.

only make psychological statements that are true by imposing the appropriate limitations on them—by saying, for instance, "For me, here and now, at my current level of consciousness, I experience the following as a fact." That is a psychologically objective assertion. It is true, but it is also a modest statement. It does not universalize one's subjectivity. This corresponds to Jung's remark that every psychological statement is a subjective confession. It is only in this way that we honor the scientific conscience and keep depth psychology from the very great danger of falling into identification with any one of a number of warring theologies and metaphysical doctrines.

Parmenides emphasizes the word *on,* the Greek word meaning "being," as contrasted with *genesia,* "becoming." Parmenides says that so far as the metaphysical dimension is concerned, there is no such thing as becoming. There is no change. There is no passing away. There is only eternal being.

When it is reflected upon, the verb "to be" has astonishing numinosity. Consider the fact that in the Old Testament, Yahweh gives his name by using that verb: "I am what I am." Descartes, when he was trying to find some bedrock reality that could not be doubted, grounded his philosophy in *Cogito ergo sum,* which can be translated as, "I am conscious, therefore I am."

Jung had an "I am" experience at about the age of twelve, as reported in his memoirs. He found himself suddenly, as if walking out of the mist, realizing that "now I am *myself!* . . . Previously . . . everything had merely happened to me . . . now *I* willed."[61]

I can remember something similar in my own boyhood, when I would repeat the word "I" over and over again until it transported me into another dimension. This experience of one's own being, the fact that "I am," opens up the greatest mystery of all. Such an experience probably lies behind Parmenides' intense preoccupation with this term, "being," such that he could not allow any contradiction of it at all.

Patients also have this experience, which can be put in clinical terms by describing the so-called "I am" experience as the repair of damage to the ego-Self axis.[62] Ordinarily one would expect to have such an experience in childhood, but sometimes one is well into adult life before having the realization that one's existence has a metaphysical substrate.

---

[61] *Memories, Dreams, Reflections*, pp. 32f.

[62] This is discussed further in my *Ego and Archetype,* pp. 56ff.

Anaxagoras

Anaxagoras, a contemporary of Parmenides, flourished about 460 B.C. He came from Clazomenae, on the coast of Asia Minor, but he lived most of his adult life in Athens, until he was exiled in old age for impiety, apparently for teaching the doctrine that the sun is a red-hot stone. His fate was similar to that of Galileo, who was excommunicated for stating that the earth was not the center of the universe.

His great contribution is the central idea of *nous,* which is always translated as "mind." Probably *nous* meant a little more than the modern term "mind" and should be translated as "consciousness." It is well to remember, however, that the early Greek mind-set was different from our own, so that translations are never exact. We have one major fragment from Anaxagoras, which includes the following passage:

> All other things partake in a portion of everything, while Nous is infinite and self-ruled, and is mixed with nothing, but is alone, itself by itself. For if it were not by itself, but were mixed with anything else, it would partake in all things if it were mixed with any; for in everything there is a portion of everything . . . and the things mixed with it would hinder it, so that it would have power over nothing in the same way that it has now being alone by itself. For it is the thinnest of all things and the purest, and it has all knowledge about everything and the greatest strength; and Nous has power over all things, both greater and smaller, that have life. And Nous had power over the whole revolution, so that it began to revolve in the beginning. And it began to revolve first from a small beginning; but the revolution now extends over a larger space, and will extend over a larger still. And all the things that are mingled together and separated off and distinguished are all known by Nous. And Nous set in order all things that were to be, and all things that were and are not now and that are, and this revolution in which now revolve the stars and the sun and the moon, and the air and the aether that are separated off. And this revolution caused the separating off, and the rare is separated off from the dense, the warm from the cold, the light from the dark, and the dry from the moist. And there are many portions in many things. But no thing is altogether separated off nor distinguished from anything else except Nous. And all Nous is alike, both the greater and the smaller; while nothing else is like anything else, but each single thing is and was most manifestly those things of which it has most in it.[63]

The basic statement is that *nous* is infinite and omniscient. Everything else in the universe is just a composite mess of separate entities, but *nous* is mixed with nothing. It is pure. The world was created when *nous* started a motion, a vortex,

---

[63] Burnet, *Greek Philosophy: Thales to Plato*, pp. 259f.

and as a consequence of that vortex, things got separated, differentiated from each other. This statement is the first major symbolic example of the process of *separatio*.[64] *Nous* is the great original, motivating, circular, revolving dynamism that separates things out and creates the universe.

The first sentence of Anaxagoras' work summarizes this idea. One should always pay attention to first sentences. Anaxagoras' reads: "All things were together. Then mind *[nous]* came and arranged them."[65]

Nous is one of the basic concepts of humanity. All the Greek philosophers used this term and elaborated it, so that it evolved over time. The word itself has been traced all the way back to Linear B, an archaic Cretan language, a precursor of Greek. The word

> probably goes back etymologically to the root *snu,* and relates to the German *schnaufen,* to pant, and *schnuppern,* to sniff. Originally it refers to the inner sense directed at an object, then, at a later time, to disposition, understanding, insight, reason, mind.[66]

The implication is that when a dog starts sniffing around, it is demonstrating the most original manifestation of *nous.* Etymology is a wonderful way of exploring the unconscious; it is the unconscious of language.

There is an anecdote told about Anaxagoras by Socrates in the *Phaedo:*

> I once heard someone reading from a book by Anaxagoras and saying that it is mind [or *nous]* which arranges and is responsible for everything. This explanation delighted me, and it seemed to me somehow to be a good thing that mind was responsible for everything—I thought that in that case mind, in arranging things, would arrange them all, and place each, in the best way possible. . . . Now, my friend, this splendid hope was dashed, for as I continued reading, I saw that the man didn't use his mind at all—he didn't ascribe to it any explanations for the arranging of things but found explanations in air and ether and water and many other absurdities.[67]

It is evident here that Socrates, as was typical also of Plato and of the ancients as a whole, identified the true with the good. There is really no reason to do that, but they did, and that opens one up to a lot of disappointments.

Originally the term *nous* meant the dynamic curiosity that sniffs out something. According to the classical scholar Bruno Snell, *nous,* with its verb, *noein,*

---

[64] For further discussion of *separatio,* see my *Anatomy of the Psyche,* chap. 7.

[65] Quoted in Barnes, *Early Greek Philosophy,* p. 236.

[66] *New International Dictionary of New Testament Theology,* vol. 3, p. 122.

[67] *Phaedo,* quoted in Barnes, *Early Greek Philosophy,* p. 235.

means "to acquire a clear image of something. . . . It is the mind as a recipient of clear images, or, more briefly, the organ of clear images."[68] Snell finds examples of its use as far back as Homer, where *nous* was attributed both to humanity and to Zeus, whose *nous* was better than humanity's; he quotes the *Iliad* (Book 16, line 688): "The *nous* of Zeus is ever stronger than that of men."

There are other terms related to *nous*, such as *noesis*, which refers to the operation of *nous* and is usually translated as "thinking." *Noeton* and *noeta*, its plural, refer to the objects of *nous*, hence to the intelligible objects. The objects that belong to the Platonic realm of ideas are the *noeta*, and the intelligible world, the world of Platonic forms, is called the *kosmos noetos*. *Pronoia* means forethought or providence, and is a term much used by the Stoics (further discussed here in chapter nine). *Ennoia* refers to a mental concept and appears in certain Gnostic doctrines as a divine being. *Dianoia* was thought or intellect or mind. *Synnoia* is equivalent to our word "consciousness"; *syn-* means "with," so *synnoia* means knowing with, or having mind with. The word *paranoia*, which in antiquity meant "madness," did not have exactly the specific flavor it has today. It had a more general meaning of madness, but it means literally "beside mind." Those are all descendants, the posterity of the word *nous*.

The central image that Anaxagoras has bequeathed us is the image of the divine transpersonal *nous* as a vortex, something like the Biblical Yahweh in the whirlwind, a dynamic manifestation of a central point which is described as the agent that creates all things through the process of *separatio*. It is like a vast cosmic centrifuging process. Originally it referred to a numinous spiritual energy that created an ordered, meaningful psychic universe through the ability to create images and initiate movement. In modern psychological terms we can consider it the dynamic, creative aspect of the Self.

A concrete illustration of such dynamic motion leading to separation is that of a container filled with pebbles of many different sizes. If one shakes such a container, a distinct layering will take place. The sand and finest particles will gather on the bottom, the small pebbles next, the larger ones next, and the big ones at the top, all in distinct layers.

---

[68] *The Discovery of Mind*, p. 13.

6
Empedocles

Empedocles, who lived about 450 B.C., is a complex and mysterious figure, originally from Sicily, who combined the features of a rational philosopher with those of a legendary shaman or magician. Like Pythagoras, he was considerably influenced by Orphism, which left a mystical strain that runs through his work. Legend tells us that he decided to turn himself into an immortal by leaping into the volcano of Etna, which is how he ended his life.

Eduard Zeller, the famous nineteenth-century historian of Greek philosophy, wrote about Empedocles:

> A wealth of legend has sprung up around his death, the best known story being his supposed leap into Aetna. The personality of Empedocles resembles that of Faust and is only to be understood if we recognize in his character the combination of a passion for scientific inquiry with a none the less passionate striving to raise himself above nature. . . . He resembles closely the miracle-workers and magicians, in that many superhuman feats were ascribed to him and his disciple Gorgias saw him at his "magic." He believed himself to be a higher being, for in the circle of birth, as physician, poet, and leader of the people, he had reached the last and highest state from which there is a return to the blissful realm of the gods; but for the moment he still wandered like an immortal god among mortals, although like them he was a "wanderer gone astray." They followed him in thousands when he passed through a city, prayed to him and asked him to show them the way that leads to salvation. . . . [His message was that] To receive this knowledge and profit by it a man needs a pure and good mind. Perhaps following a precedent of the Pythagoreans he first communicated his doctrines to his disciples only under a vow of secrecy. He expounded them in two poems, which far from being mutually contradictory are the products of one and the same mind.[69]

One of the poems was called *On Nature (Physis),* and the other was *Purifications (Katharses).* His best-known doctrine concerning the nature of things is summarized by Barnes: *"On Nature* described a complex, cyclical history of the universe. Everything is compounded from four elements or 'roots.' "[70]

The Greek word for root is *rhizomata.* The word "elements" *(stoicheia)* was not in use yet but was applied to his doctrine later; the word he used was *rhi-*

[69] *Outlines of the History of Greek Philosophy,* pp. 70f.

[70] *Early Greek Philosophy,* p. 165.

zomata. In addition to the four *rhizomata,* there are two primary moving factors: love *(philia)* and strife *(neikos).* These elements are subject to a cyclic process in which they periodically unite into a divine and homogeneous sphere. The sphere then dissolves, and by this the world is established in a series of stages. Then the cycle reverses, and the universe gradually returns to the state of the sphere. This cosmic cycle rolls on repeatedly without beginning or end. Empedocles says: "Hear first the four roots of all things: bright Zeus, life-bringing Hera, Aidoneus, and Nestis, who waters with her tears the mortal fountains."[71]

Nestis was a Sicilian water goddess; the other three are more familiar: Zeus, Hera and Hades. Various commentators have related different elements to the four deities. Here, Zeus will be fire, Hera earth, Hades air, and Nestis water.[72] It is historically interesting that the four *rhizomata* have the names of deities. Empedocles' poem is a good example of a transition stage in which philosophical concepts are still mixed with their personified, mythological origins. It demonstrates quite explicitly Cornford's contention that the original categories of early Greek philosophy came right out of Greek religion and mythology.

Empedocles' work is the first example in which there are thought to be four *arche;* previously there was a single one. In Empedocles' philosophical myth we see the archetypal ordering principle of the quaternity functioning as a world creator. The quaternity stamps its fourfold nature onto the original undifferentiated stuff. This is an example of projection in the early development of the psyche: out of the original undifferentiated unconscious, the fourfold pattern orders the emerging psyche.

In addition to the four material substances, Empedocles also talks about two dynamic principles—*philia* and *neikos.* He considers that there is a cyclic alternation between these two principles. The alternation can be looked upon as a movement between the processes of *separatio,* brought about by strife and opposition, and those of *coniunctio,* the connecting of all the elements of the universe, brought about by love. The image is that of a great homogeneous sphere—this is the nature of the universe—in which all things are undifferentiated and bound together by *philia,* which is what the alchemists called the world glue, one of the names for their arcane substance.

Gradually *philia* streams out of the sphere, and, according to certain early texts, deadly *neikos* streams in and takes its place. This starts to bring about a

---

[71] Ibid., pp. 173f.

[72] See also a description by Hippolytus in *The Refutation of All Heresies,* in Alexander Roberts and James Donaldson, eds., *The Ante-Nicene Fathers,* vol. 5, pp. 110ff.

separation of things. As the homogeneous sphere undergoes fragmentation, dismemberment and breakup into different entities, the visible world is created. It is a cosmogonic process that is brought about by *neikos,* so that *neikos* is the Demiurge, the world creator. This idea is analogous to the cosmology of the Gnostics, in which the world is created by the evil one, by strife, which by most standards is considered evil. Anything that separates carries a negative quality.

The visible world and its multitude of objects is thus created out of the original homogeneous sphere, and after a time the process reverses itself. *Philia* starts to reassert its prominence, bringing all things back together. The homogeneous sphere is recreated under the rule of love, and so on, indefinitely.

This is quite an impressive image, which has no basis in external reality. Since there is no external reference for it, it is better seen as a projected picture of the psychic development of the individual ego as it emerges during the fragmentation of the original state of unconscious wholeness. Then, when that multitudinous ego has reached a certain stage of development, individuation proper starts to operate. If this proceeds, it achieves a renewal of the original state of spherical wholeness, but on another level of consciousness.

This is the basic doctrine of Empedocles' work entitled *On Nature.* In his other work, *Purifications (Katharses),* there is pictured a similar cyclic movement in the universe on the part of the souls that move in and out of visible, earthly existence—an Orphic doctrine. The main theme of *Purifications* is the fall of souls from an original state of blessedness. Because of crimes they have committed, they are condemned to a series of earthly existences until such time as they have purified themselves. This is elaborated by F.M. Cornford:

> The basis of Empedocles' position is disclosed in the famous fragment describing the exile of the soul and its wanderings round the wheel of rebirth:
>
> "There is an oracle of Necessity, a decree of the Gods from of old, everlasting, with broad oaths fast sealed, that, whensoever one of the daemons, whose portion is length of days, has sinfully stained his hands with blood, or followed Strife *[neikos]* and sworn a false oath, he must wander thrice ten thousand seasons away from the Blessed, being born throughout the time in all manner of mortal forms, passing from one to another of the painful paths of life.
>
> For the power of the Air drives him seaward; and the Sea spews him out on the dry land; Earth hurls him into the rays of the blazing Sun, and Sun into the eddies of Air. One from another receives him, and he is loathed of all.
>
> Of these now am I also one, an exile from God and a wanderer, having put my trust in raging Strife."[73]

---

[73] *From Religion to Philosophy,* p. 228.

The idea of being an alien in the universe is a Gnostic doctrine, which has its roots in this ancient source. Cornford continues:

> The doctrine can be classed unhesitatingly as "Orphic." The soul is conceived as falling from the region of light down into the "roofed-in Cave," the "dark meadow of *Ate* [fate, delusion or folly]." This fall is a penalty for sin—flesh-eating or oath-breaking. Caught in the wheel of Time, the soul, preserving its individual identity, passes through all shapes of life. . . . Its substance is divine and immutable, and it is the same substance as all other soul in the world. In this sense, the unity of all life is maintained; but, on the other hand, each soul is an atomic individual, which persists throughout its ten thousand years' cycle of reincarnations. The soul travels the round of the four elements. . . .
>
> The soul is further called "an exile from God and a wanderer," and its offense, which entailed this exile, is described as "following Strife," "putting trust in Strife." At the end of the cycle of births, men may hope to "appear among mortals as prophets, song-writers, physicians, and princes; and thence they rise up, as Gods exalted in honor, sharing the hearth of the other immortals and the same table, free from human woes, delivered from destiny and harm." Thus the course of the soul begins with separation from God, and ends in reunion with him, after passing through all the moirai [all the various portions] of the elements.[74]

This passage is a projected image of ego development. The soul coming out of the blessed state down to earthly existence corresponds to the birth of the ego out of the blissful paradise state of the Garden of Eden—the unconscious before the birth of consciousness. The birth of consciousness is accompanied by a crime, and various processes are set up to expiate the ego or purify it from the crimes it commits in the course of setting itself up as an autonomous center of being. It is a crime against the universe for the ego to exist, and since it finds itself in that impure state, it has to undergo *katharsis*. The Orphics, the Pythagoreans, and very probably the Empedocleans as well, took this idea of purity very concretely indeed. One was not to eat meat, for instance, because there was a common soul substance in all living entities. To eat meat was to murder a fellow soul.

Katharsis is a word that is important for the contemporary idea of consciousness. With a somewhat different interpretation of the word *katharos* (pure), we can quite properly say that the analytic process is a purification. One who is pure psychologically is conscious of his own "dirt." Purity, psychologically speaking, has a much more refined and subtle meaning than the purity of the Puritans, which involves rampant shadow projection. Psychological purity means shadow

---

[74] Ibid., p. 229.

integration: the really pure person is conscious of his own impurities.

The evolution of the word *katharsis* is interesting. *Katharos,* which is its root, originally meant clean in the physical sense, like clean water as opposed to dirty water. By the time of Homer, and certainly by the time of the Old Testament, the word had come to mean ritually—not physically—clean. In ritual terms being unclean meant that one had touched or had dealings with taboo objects and thus needed to be cleansed. There was no moral dimension yet, just a ritual one. In later, more developed religious terms, by the time of Jeremiah, for instance, the idea of purity becomes one of moral purity. It is no longer a matter of being circumcised physically but rather of having a circumcised heart, so to speak. Here, "heart" can be understood as the equivalent of psyche. This is a much more developed notion of purity, but it still involves notable shadow projection.

A further development is seen by the time of the Pyramid Texts in Egypt. When the deceased arrives in the afterworld and has to prove his right to continued existence, he has to give a negative confession, in which he announces: I never oppressed the widows and the orphans, I never stole, etc., going through all the various crimes that he did not do, in order to establish his moral purity, something beyond ritual purity.

Greek and Hebrew concepts of purity were in some contrast. In Greek there is just the one major word for pure, *katharos.* When the Old Testament was translated into Greek in the third century, the word *katharos* was used for eighteen different Hebrew equivalents. That shows how important the concept of purity was for the ancient Israelites. It had much less emphasis in Greece, except for the Orphics and for the philosophers who were influenced by the Orphics, especially Pythagoras and Empedocles.[75]

Peters describes how the usage of the word *katharsis* evolved among the Greek philosophers. Very early, the literal, physical and ritual usage shifted and the word came to express purification of the soul by rendering it harmonious through the use of philosophy. By the time of Socrates the function of *katharsis* is the removal of evil from the soul, as the medical art removes toxins from the body. A cathartic, for example, cleans the digestive tract of its lingering debris. Socrates thought of philosophy as doing something analogous for the soul and putting it into harmony; thus, the soul is cleansed of false opinions by means of Socrates' purgative interrogation. Aristotle uses the term in relation to the effect of the tragic drama. He speaks of it as a purgation of the soul of pity and fear,

---

[75] See *New International Dictionary of New Testament Theology,* vol. 3, pp. 102f.

which is a still more complex and subtle idea.[76]

Empedocles continues to live in the collective psyche. Just as Thales shows up in Part Two of Goethe's *Faust,* Empedocles shows up as a prominent figure in the work of three major poets of the nineteenth century: Hölderlin, Matthew Arnold and Nietzsche. It is significant that all three of these poets, who were gripped by the image and the life of Empedocles, were also preoccupied with the modern despair which accompanies the loss of our religious myth. These poets were about a hundred years ahead of their time. In the nineteenth century, although the majority of people did not know it, our functioning myth was already in its death throes. Each of these three poets perceived Empedocles as a transition figure who lived, as they did, between two different ages. Empedocles does have this double strand in his work: on the one hand, he looks back to the religious Orphic conception of existence; on the other, he looks forward to the rational scientific image of the universe, which began to emerge in ancient Greece.

In Hölderlin's poem, Empedocles describes his childhood experiences and then he goes on to say:

> So quietly I grew up, and other things
> Already were prepared. More forcefully yet,
> Like water, did the savage human wave
> Beat on my breast, and the poor people's voice,
> Humming in blind confusion, reach my ear.
> And when, while silent in my room I sat,
> At midnight tumult and revolt cry out,
> And through the fields they rush, and weary of life
> With their own hands break up their own good houses
> And temples, long made odious, and forsaken,
> When brothers fled each other, men hurried past
> Those they loved most, and fathers no longer knew
> Their sons, and human language had become
> Incomprehensible, and human law,
> The meaning of it, shivering me, struck home:
> It was the departure of my people's god!
> Him I could hear, and up to the silent planet
> Whence he had come to us, I turned my gaze.
> And to propitiate him I set out.
> Still many happy a day was granted us.
> Still, in the end, renewal seemed at hand;
> And, my mind fixed upon the golden age,
> When trust was general, that bright, strong morning,

---

[76] Peters, *Greek Philosophical Terms*, p. 98.

My gloom, the people's terrible gloom, dispersed
And we made pacts as firm as they were free,
And once again invoked the living gods.
Yet often, when the people's gratitude
Crowned me with wreaths, and ever closer to me,
To me alone, the people's soul drew, quickly
It dawned on me: that where a land must die
The Spirit at the last elects one more
Through whom the swansong, the last life, shall sound.
Well I divined it, yet I served him gladly.
Now it is done. And nevermore shall I
Belong to mortals. O my evening time![77]

This poem tells us very powerfully how Hölderlin saw the end of Western civilization. He also paid the price; he fell into a psychosis and was insane for the last thirty-six years of his life, which helps to account for his fascination with the image of Empedocles jumping into the fiery volcano.

Nietzsche had a somewhat similar identification. He, too, spent the last years of his life in psychosis, gripped with the realization that God is dead. He identified with Empedocles quite directly, as indicated in his autobiography:

I have tried to turn philosophy into an art—the art of living. With this goal in mind I followed the example of Empedocles of Agrigentum and sought to organize all knowledge into a single whole, to harmonize with the symphony of the planets. . . . But since there was no love in my age or in my private life, I could not conceive of any cosmic Love [philia] rooted in man's members, as Empedocles put it, and the cosmic conflict between love and strife which harmonized itself in the process of dynamic living, became for me strife alone, the sheer brutality of social Darwinism. It was Lou Salome who pounded away at her Tolstoyan thesis of love's hegemony over hate, a thesis that Empedocles himself expounded and in which I lost faith when I was exposed as a child to the frost-bitten Puritanism of Naumburg with its chilling atmosphere of prudery and decorum.

In her arms I could well believe with Empedocles that cosmic love was rooted in my own members and vouched for itself. . . .

The legend-makers saw Empedocles plunging into the belching flames of Aetna, but this fate was reserved not for the great pre-Socratic, but for me alone. Having been separated from the love of my life, the love that made me human, I made my desperate plunge into the fires of madness, hoping like Zarathustra to snatch faith in myself by going out of my mind and entering a higher region of sanity—the sanity of the raving lunatic, the normal madness of the damned![78]

---

[77] "Empedocles," in Friedrich Hölderlin, *Poems and Fragments,* pp. 357f.

[78] *My Sister and I,* p. 113.

The third example is Matthew Arnold, who wrote a poem entitled, "Empedocles on Etna." He had a different psychology from these other two. He was sound psychologically but keenly aware of the desperate consequences of the death of our collective myth. His poem "Dover Beach" is a threnody for our lost myth. In another poem, "Stanzas from 'The Grand Chartreuse,' " he wrote:

> Wandering between two worlds, one dead,
> The other powerless to be born,
> With nowhere yet to rest my head,
> Like these, on earth I wait forlorn.[79]

Arnold saw in Empedocles a partner who had lived through the forlorn transition between the death of one god and the birth of another.

In Nietzsche's *Thus Spake Zarathustra,* there is a passage in which Zarathustra descends into a volcano. Jung did not know Nietzsche's autobiography, but in a seminar on him he speaks about the image of the descent into the volcano:

> Of course Nietzsche must have known—he was a classical philologist—that Empedocles, the great philosopher, had chosen that form of death for himself: he jumped into the flaming crater of Aetna. I often wonder why he did it. A Latin poet said about him that it was in order to be considered an immortal god. But in the biography of old Empedocles we get the real clue! You know, he was very popular: wherever he appeared, large crowds of people came to hear him talk, and when he left town about ten thousand people followed him to the next one where he had to talk again. I assume he was human, so what could he do? He had to find a place where the ten thousand people would not run after him, so he jumped into Aetna. It had nothing to do with being an immortal god, but was just in order to have his peace.[80]

---

[79] *Poetry and Criticism of Matthew Arnold,* p. 187.

[80] *Nietzsche's Zarathustra,* vol. 2, p. 1217.

7

Socrates and Plato

Socrates lived in Athens from about 470 to 399 B.C. and Plato from 427 to 347 B.C. It is almost impossible to know for certain which writings derive from Socrates and which from Plato. Emerson called them a "double star which the most powerful instruments will not entirely separate."[81] It is possible, however, to distinguish their differing personalities.

Plato was the scion of a prominent Athenian family, with all the virtues and elitist tendencies of the aristocracy. He was an introverted thinking type. Socrates, on the other hand, was a commoner. His father was a stonecutter and his mother a midwife. He himself was a talker, an extrovert, not a writer. His constant concern was in making personal connections with the young men of Athens, usually very aristocratic young men. Those connections often had an erotic overlay. He spent his days in the *agora* in endless dialogue with bright young men. In spite of his rationality, one can recognize him as an eros man.

Two concepts clearly belong to the life and experience of Socrates rather than of Plato. They are represented by the terms *daimonion* and *maieusis*. *Daimonion* means "little daimon." The word is the root of what has become, in English, the word "demon," but negative associations did not apply to it in antiquity. *Daimon* referred to a divinity-like entity that manifested itself through the human soul. On a number of occasions, Socrates states that he has an inner *daimon*. This is usually translated "sign" or "voice," or sometimes "oracle." This inner *daimon* warned him when he was in danger of doing the wrong thing. In the dialogue *Apology,* he tells the judges at his trial:

> O my judges . . . I should like to tell you of a wonderful circumstance. Hitherto the divine faculty of which the internal oracle is the source has constantly been in the habit of opposing me even about trifles, if I was going to make a slip or error in any matter; and now as you see there has come upon me that which may be thought, and is generally believed to be, the last and worst evil. But the oracle made no sign of opposition, either when I was leaving my house in the morning, or when I was on my way to the court, or while I was speaking, at anything which I was going to say; and yet I have often been stopped in the middle of a speech, but now in nothing I either said or did touching the matter in hand has the oracle op-

---

[81] "Plato; or, The Philosopher" (from *Representative Men),* in *The Selected Writings of Ralph Waldo Emerson,* p. 488.

posed me. What do I take to be the explanation of this silence? I will tell you. It is an intimation that what has happened to me is a good, and that those of us who think that death is an evil are in error. For the customary sign *[daimonion]* would surely have opposed me had I been going to evil and not to good.[82]

The inner *daimon* is discussed in other dialogues in much the same way. This experience, of course, is completely familiar to a depth psychologist, mainly in terms of dreams. Often one will anticipate a certain action and will have a clear-cut warning dream that says in so many words, "Don't do that." But if one is in good enough relation to the unconscious, one does not have to wait for a dream. The Socratic *daimon* will speak from within. It is a trans-ego phenomenon that operates on the margin of consciousness, which can be understood, of course, as a function of the Self, the greater personality within. When the ego is in the right relation to it, it functions like a guardian angel.

The other term unique to Socrates is *maieusis,* midwifery. Socrates' mother was a midwife, and he applied the term to himself:

My art of midwifery is in general like theirs; the only difference is that my patients are men, not women, and my concern is not with the body but with the soul that is in travail of birth. And the highest point of my art is the power to prove by every test whether the offspring of a young man's thought is a false phantom or instinct with life and truth. I am so far like the midwife that I cannot myself give birth to wisdom, and the common reproach is true, that, though I question others, I can myself bring nothing to light because there is no wisdom in me. The reason is this. Heaven constrains me to serve as a midwife, but has debarred me from giving birth. So of myself I have no sort of wisdom, nor has any discovery ever been born to me as the child of my soul. Those who frequent my company at first appear, some of them, quite unintelligent, but, as we go further with our discussions, all who are favored by heaven make progress at a rate that seems surprising to others, as well as to themselves, although it is clear that they have never learned anything from me. The many admirable truths they bring to birth have been discovered by themselves from within. But the delivery is heaven's work and mine.

The proof of this is that many who have not been conscious of my assistance but have made light of me, thinking it was all their own doing, have left me sooner than they should, whether under others' influence or of their own motion, and thenceforward suffered miscarriage of their thoughts through falling into bad company, and they have lost the children of whom I had delivered them by bringing them up badly, caring more for false phantoms than for the true. And so at last their lack of understanding has become apparent to themselves and to everyone else. . . . When they come back and beg for a renewal of our intercourse with extravagant protestations, sometimes the divine warning that comes to me forbids it;

---

[82] *Apology,* sec. 40, in B. Jowett, trans., *The Dialogues of Plato,* pp. 421f.

with others it is permitted, and these begin again to make progress. In yet another way those who seek my company have the same experience as a woman with child; they suffer the pains of labor and, by night and day, are full of distress far greater than a woman's, and my art has power to bring on these pangs or to allay them.[83]

He could have been talking about analysis. Analysis owes a lot to Socrates in terms of practical procedure. Jung remarks as early as 1912: "Analysis is a refined technique of Socratic maieutics."[84]

Marie-Louise von Franz discusses the psychology of Socrates in her essay "The Dream of Socrates."[85] This study, written when she was quite young, is critical of him for lacking anima development and for being identified with the mother. Of course these qualities were characteristic of the ancient Greeks as a whole, but Socrates stood out among his contemporaries, and modern standards should not be applied to him. Probably von Franz's interpretation was intended more or less consciously to apply to modern young men who tend to identify with Socratic rationalism, in which case the criticisms are quite apt. But in regard to the historical Socrates she misses the mark, because his psychological depth, for a man of his time and place, is the most important feature about him. One cannot talk about his personal psychology without acknowledging that fact.

The other member of the double star of Greek philosophy is Plato. As a member of an Athenian family with a long history of prominence in public affairs, Plato's initial intention was to follow the tradition and go into politics himself. However, he was bitterly disillusioned by events at the end of the Peloponesian War, and when he came under the influence of Socrates his true introverted nature had a chance to flower.

Alfred North Whitehead has said that all of Western philosophy is no more than a series of footnotes to Plato, but Emerson's appreciation of the man was perhaps the finest of all. In *Representative Men,* he includes an essay on Plato as the representative philosopher. It brings in the feeling dimension, which is important when approaching individuals of this magnitude:

Among secular books, Plato only is entitled to Omar's fanatical compliment to the Koran, when he said, "Burn the libraries; for their value is in this book." These sentences contain the culture of nations; these are the corner-stone of schools; these are the fountain-head of literatures. . . . There was never such a range of

---

[83] *Theatetus*, sec. 150b-e, in Hamilton and Cairns, *Plato's Collected Dialogues*, p. 855.

[84] "The Theory of Psychoanalysis," *Freud and Psychoanalysis,* CW 4, par. 519.

[85] *Dreams*, pp. 35-64.

speculation. Out of Plato come all things that are still written and debated among men of thought. Great havoc makes he among our originalities. We have reached the mountain from which all these drift boulders were detached. The Bible of the learned for twenty-two hundred years, every brisk young man who says in succession fine things to each reluctant generation . . . is some reader of Plato, translating into the vernacular, wittily, his good things. Even the men of grander proportion suffer some deduction from the misfortune (shall I say?) of coming after this exhausting generalizer. . . .

Plato is philosophy, and philosophy, Plato—at once the glory and the shame of mankind, since neither Saxon nor Roman have availed to add any idea to his categories. No wife, no children had he, and the thinkers of all civilized nations are his posterity and are tinged with his mind. How many great men Nature is incessantly sending up out of night, to be *his men*—Platonists! the Alexandrians, a constellation of genius; the Elizabethans. . . .Calvinism is in his *Phaedo*. Christianity is in it. Mahometanism draws all its philosophy . . . from him. Mysticism finds in Plato all of its texts. This citizen of a town in Greece is no villager nor patriot. An Englishman reads and says "how English!" A German—"how Teutonic!" An Italian— "how Roman and how Greek!" As they say that Helen of Argos had that universal beauty that everybody felt related to her, so Plato seems to a reader in New England an American genius. His broad humanity transcends all sectional lines.[86]

Needless to say, Emerson is known as the American Platonist.

It is impossible to do justice to the massive bulk of Plato's writings in a single essay. But we must acknowledge two central terms. The first is *eidos* (plural *eide),* which derives from the Greek verb *eido* meaning to see or to know. *Eidos* is translated as "idea," "form" or "original pattern." The idea is particularly significant to Jungian psychology, because it is the precursor of the concept of the archetype. Eduard Zeller describes the nature of the *eide:*

The Heraclitan world of coming into being and ceasing to be, with its eternal changeableness, cannot be an object of knowledge. There must be another world which . . . answers to the demands of permanence and durability without which there can be no knowledge. The former is the world of sense perception, the latter the world of thought. Thought fixes its attention not on what is peculiar in things but on the general, that which is common to all things which belong to a "kind" of being. Thus it is not the particular in each separate thing that is lasting and essential but that which it has in common with other things of its kind. This common quality, which since Aristotle we call the concept, was termed by Plato the idea [eidos].[87]

Zeller goes on to speak about mathematics as an example of *eidos:*

---

[86] *Selected Writings,* pp. 471f.

[87] *Outlines of the History of Greek Philosophy,* p. 147.

The form of a square, for example, is fixed once and for all, however many individual examples of the figure may exist. All these individual figures are only squares in so far as the square form is present in them or they participate in it. Everything else about them is insignificant for the idea of the square. . . . For Plato the non-sensual nature of things is the only true reality, which is to be distinguished from their sensual phenomena. The ideas are for him not mere things of thought . . . but realities. There are ideas of everything possible: not merely of things, but of qualities too. . . . The ideas form a world [that world was called the *kosmos noitos,* the world of the *nous]* which exists of itself, is eternal and unchanging and can only be comprehended by thought. In this pure and independent existence they have their abode in a "super-celestial" place, where the soul in its pre-existence has perceived them. All learning and knowledge consists in the recollection by the soul of the ideas when it perceives the things of sense. The earthly sensually perceptible things are mere shadowy images of the bright world of ideas, a view which finds clear and emphatic expression in the famous simile of the cave at the beginning of the seventh book of the *Republic.*[88]

Plato is perhaps best known for this simile of the cave, pictured opposite, which is quite relevant to depth psychology. Plato says in the *Republic:*

Picture men dwelling in a sort of subterranean cavern with a long entrance open to the light on its entire width. Conceive them as having their legs and necks fettered from childhood, so that they remain in the same spot, able to look forward only, and prevented by the fetters from turning their heads. Picture further the light from a fire burning higher up and at a distance behind them, and between the fire and the prisoners and above them a road along which a low wall has been built, as the exhibitors of puppet shows have partitions before the men themselves, above which they show the puppets. . . .

See also, then, men carrying past the wall implements of all kinds that rise above the wall, and human images and shapes of animals as well. . . .

[This is] like to us, I said. For, to begin with, tell me do you think that these men would have seen anything of themselves or of one another except the shadows cast from the fire on the wall of the cave that fronted them? How could they, he said, if they were compelled to hold their heads unmoved through life?

 . . . . If then they were able to talk to one another, do you not think that they would suppose that in naming the things that they saw they were naming the passing objects? Necessarily.

And if their prison had an echo from the wall opposite them, when one of the passersby uttered a sound, do you think that they would suppose anything else than the passing shadow to be the speaker? . . . Then in every way such prisoners would deem reality to be nothing else than the shadows of the artificial objects.[89]

---

[88] Ibid., pp. 147f.

[89] *Republic,* book 7, 514, in Hamilton and Cairns, *Plato's Collected Dialogues,* p. 747.

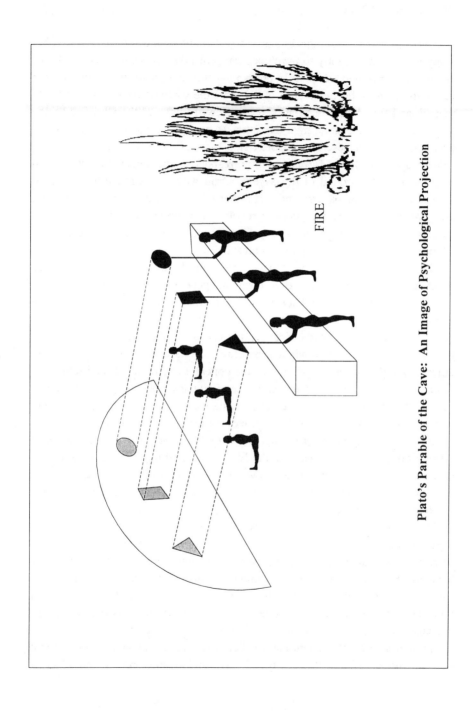

FIRE

Plato's Parable of the Cave: An Image of Psychological Projection

Plato, of course, meant this image to apply to our view of external reality, but it applies even more aptly to psychological projection. It is almost as if Plato's imagination invented the picture projector—the slide projector or the motion picture projector—far in advance of his time: the source of light is in the background, and the objects in front of the source of light cast their images on the screen, precisely the same light dynamics as a picture projector. This is also a very apt image to describe psychological projection. The parade of figures holding up the different forms would correspond to the archetypal actions and actors in the background of the psyche. Ordinarily, one's attention is not directed to the psychic background, but rather to the external world, and so what one perceives in the external world is regularly contaminated with the archetypal dramas which are going on internally. They appear to be outside, taking place in relation to other people and outer circumstances.

The notion of these Platonic "ideas" grew out of mankind's early experience of discovering the mind's power to formulate general categories. It is very hard now for us to put ourselves back into those earlier stages of consciousness, but one gets some idea of them through anthropological studies of primitives who do not generalize; they have concrete experiences. For the Greeks, the powers of generalization were just slowly and painfully emerging from the universal condition of *participation mystique* with the concrete environment, and therefore, when a generalization was discovered, it carried the same numinosity as the discovery of numbers. Numbers are generalizations, which is why Plato used them as prime examples to describe the nature of the idea. Numbers are *eide*.

Likewise it is a big step from dealing with, say, individual dogs to the realization of dog nature in general, to the Platonic idea of dog. It is an even bigger step to move from concern about individual experiences of good fortune or honest, fair treatment to the formulation of the generalities (or Platonic ideas) of the Good itself or of Justice itself.

This same process is seen in modern psychotherapy, involving not intellectual categories, but the categories of psychological experience. Suppose, for example, that a patient has an angry or contemptuous reaction to someone else's behavior. He then dreams that a criminal has taken up residence in his house. The analyst, in interpreting that dream and relating it to the behavior, would point out that the patient has encountered his shadow, that his reaction to his colleague is a projection, a shadow projection.

Another example: a patient has a sullen, resentful mood, and he dreams that he is having an affair with a shady lady. The analyst interprets the mood as an experience of his regressive anima. When there have been a number of such interpretive occasions and the patient begins to recognize his shadow and his anima, a psychological process of generalization has taken place. It is really a significant step forward in consciousness to move from individual occasions of possession by a mood or an affect, to a realization—a generalization—that they are all particular experiences of the same internal psychological figure.

The second central Platonic term is *anamnesis,* which is translated as remembrance or recollection. The basic idea is that knowledge of the *eide* existed before we were born and that this knowledge can be recovered through *anamnesis,* through recollection. This is spoken of in the *Phaedo.* Socrates refers to the fact that certain concepts like equality are examples of the *eidos,* and says that we must have had knowledge of absolute "equality" even before we had any particular examples to illustrate it. And so we must have acquired the knowledge of the idea "equal" at some time previous, and that would have to have been before we were born. And if we acquired this knowledge before we were born, and we were born having it, then we also knew at the instant of birth, not only the idea of "equal," but all the other ideas, too, like "beauty," "the good," "justice" and "holiness." He continues:

> But if the knowledge which we acquired before birth was lost by us at birth, and if afterwards by the use of our senses we recovered what we previously knew, will not the process which we call learning be a recovering of the knowledge which is natural to us, and may not this be rightly termed *anamnesis?*[90]

One can see here both the basic formula and the Socratic method. In one of the other dialogues, the *Meno,* Socrates takes an illiterate slave boy of one of his companions and demonstrates by asking him questions that the slave boy knows the Pythagorean theorem, but he does not know that he knows it. In that way he shows that he is not pouring wisdom into a person; he is just educing it, which is what the word "education" means. He is drawing it out from what one would call the unconscious, because the person knew it all the time; he just had to be reminded of it.

In medicine, treatment of a patient regularly begins by taking what is called an anamnesis, which is also done preliminary to psychotherapy. The whole lengthy examination of childhood experience is a Platonic *anamnesis,* a deliberate evoking and recollection of the experience that was once conscious to the patient and that needs to be recalled. By this process one promotes the integra-

---

[90] *Phaedo,* sec. 75, in Jowett, *The Dialogues of Plato,* p. 460.

tion of the personal unconscious, If the process goes on, the collective unconscious opens up. Then the anamnesis takes on an historical dimension beyond the lifespan of the patient as archetypal images emerge: recollections of the race, innate knowledge or patterns that are built into the collective unconscious. These could in a sense be called prenatal, at least insofar as the ego is concerned.

In reading the *Phaedo* one cannot avoid being impressed with Plato's idea of the immortality of the soul *(anima)*. Socrates argues for the immortality of the soul by suggesting that the soul must return to where it came from in order to replenish the soul substance. This introduces the image of circulation:

> Here is a new way by which we arrive at the conclusion that the living come from the dead, just as the dead come from the living. . . . If generation were in a straight line only, and there were no compensation or circle in nature, no turn or return of elements into their opposites, then you know that all things would at last have the same form and pass into the same state, and there would be no more generation of them.
>
>   . . . If all things which partook of life were to die, and after they were dead remained in the form of death, and did not come to life again, all would at last die, and nothing would be alive—what other result could there be? For if the living spring from any other things, and they too die, must not all things at last be swallowed up in death?[91]

The basic image is that of the circulation of soul substance, the image of the uroboros. Although the rational argument may leave something to be desired, behind the argument one can see that a primordially apt image is being described. But Plato does not stop with just a simple process of circulation. There is the further idea that a judgment takes place after death, complicating the circulation process:

> But then, O my friends, he said, if the soul is really immortal, what care should be taken of her, not only in respect of the portion of time which is called life, but of eternity! And the danger of neglecting her from this point of view does indeed appear to be awful. If death had only been the end of all, the wicked would have had a good bargain in dying, for they would have been happily quit not only of their body, but of their own evil together with their souls. But now, inasmuch as the soul is manifestly immortal, there is no release or salvation from evil except the attainment of the highest virtue and wisdom. For the soul when on her progress to the world below takes nothing with her but nurture and education; and these are said greatly to benefit or greatly to injure the departed, at the very beginning of his journey thither.

---

[91] Ibid., sec. 72, pp. 455f.

For after death, as they say, the genius of each individual, to whom he belonged in life, leads him to a certain place in which the dead are gathered together, whence after judgment has been given they pass into the world below, following the guide, who is appointed to conduct them from this world to the other: and when they have there received their due and remained their time, another guide brings them back again after many revolutions of the ages.[92]

After describing in some detail that other world, he continues:

Such is the nature of the other world; and when the dead arrive at the place to which the genius of each severally guides them, first of all, they have sentence passed upon them, as they have lived well and piously or not. And those who appear to have lived neither well nor ill, go to the River Acheron, and embarking in any vessels which they may find, are carried in them to the lake, and there they dwell and are purified of their evil deeds, and having suffered the penalty of the wrongs which they have done to others, they are absolved, and receive the rewards of their good deeds, each of them according to their deserts. But those who appear to be incurable by reason of the greatness of their crimes—who have committed many and terrible deeds of sacrilege, murders foul and violent, or the like—such are hurled into Tartarus which is their suitable destiny, and they never come out. . . Those too who have been pre-eminent for holiness of life are released from this earthly prison, and go to their pure home which is above, and dwell in the purer earth; and of these, such as have duly purified themselves with philosophy live henceforth altogether without the body, in mansions fairer still, which may not be described, and of which the time would fail me to tell.[93]

This passage reflects the influence of Orphic doctrine on Plato, and it is the source of the Catholic doctrine of Purgatory and Hell. It is given more complete elaboration in the "Myth of Er," described in the last book of the *Republic*. Er was a warrior who was left for dead on the battlefield, and after some days he came back to life and reported his after-death experiences. A lengthy description follows of the nature of the other world, similar to the one Socrates elaborates in the *Phaedo*.

This example, along with the other material, illustrates Nietzsche's epigram that "Christianity is Platonism for 'the people.' "[94] His insight rings true today. From a psychological point of view, Plato's system (and Christian dogma) are projec-tions of the individuation process onto the afterlife. The postmortem judgment scene is an image of the occasion on which the ego is required to con-

---

[92] Ibid., sec. 107, p. 497.

[93] Ibid., secs. 113f., pp. 497f.

[94] "Beyond Good and Evil," in *Basic Writings of Nietzsche,* p. 193.

front its shadow. The Greek psyche was so remote from the conscious recognition of the shadow that the experience was projected completely into the postmortem life.

A related Platonic idea is of a circulation of soul substance in which egos are born into the world of sensory existence, and must live a certain way during their incarnated period in order to meet the requirements of the afterlife. This does have built into it the implication that the soul substance is undergoing a differentiating or purifying process.

Jung's work communicates hints of an analogous idea. Jung does not spell this out specifically, but an effort to make it more specific appears in my book *The Creation of Consciousness.*[95] The working hypothesis there is that there is a circulation of soul substance, of psyche, which is born into the material world in the form of specific individual egos. These individuals carry manifestations of the archetypal psyche, and have the potential for progressive transformation. This is necessary for the transformation of the paradoxical God-image through human consciousness. It is possible that as the individual ego undergoes the process of individuation, a deposit or a residue of that ego's life is deposited in the archetypal psyche in transformed form. It is a little piece of the paradoxical God-image that has circulated through a conscious human ego and has undergone transformation. One can see the totality of the human enterprise as promoting that process of divine transformation. The roots of the image go back to Plato and even earlier.

---

[95] Pp. 23ff.

8
Aristotle

Aristotle was born in 384 B.C. in Macedonia, north of Greece, and grew up in the court as the son of the king's physician. At 18, he came to Athens and became a student of Plato, and remained there for twenty years. After Plato's death in 347 B.C., Aristotle left Athens and for several years was the tutor of young Alexander of Macedon, whom we know as Alexander the Great. Then, at 49, he returned to Athens, where he formed what is called the Peripatetic school of philosophy, which he headed for twelve years. After Alexander's death in 323 B.C., there was an outburst of anti-Macedonian feeling in Athens, and even though Aristotle did not have any overt political involvement, his association with Alexander and his Macedonian roots put him in a difficult position. He left Athens to retire to the island of Euboea, near mainland Greece, where he died a year later, in 322 B.C., at the age of 62.

His connection with Alexander the Great is symbolically significant. Aristotle, arriving last in the sequence of the Greek philosophers, represents the triumph of the ego. He was a world conqueror intellectually, every bit as much as Alexander was politically and militarily. In a certain sense they shared the same psychology. In Aristotle we see the full emergence of the conscious rational ego. This also means that he does not have as much to offer psychological scrutiny as most of the other philosophers, because he concentrates so much on the conscious level. With Aristotle, ego-consciousness starts splitting itself off in a major way from its archetypal background.

One of Aristotle's major accomplishments was his work on logic. He taught humanity how to think objectively and how to understand nature. Objective, scientific investigation substantially begins with him. These functions belong to the symbol system of *separatio,* that aspect of consciousness which emphasizes discriminating one thing from another, classifying and categorizing.

Aristotle even speaks about psychology in his treatise on the psyche, entitled, in Latin, *De Anima* (Concerning the Soul), and in Greek *Peri Psyche* (Concerning the Psyche). It is the first full-scale objective effort to study psychology. Many of the questions it raises remain unanswered to this day and are still a matter of concern.

In *De Anima* Aristotle asks the question, "What is the psyche?" It still cannot be adequately defined. He inquires, is there a collective or universal psyche, as well as an individual one? What is the relation between psyche and soma—between soul and body? Can the psyche exist without connection to a body? Is the psyche the source of movement (psychologically this would mean, is it the source of intention, of volition?), or is the psyche moved by some prior agent, namely God? The answer may be obvious, but the more one reflects on it, the more uncertain one becomes about the seed of our motivation and energy.

To put the question in more modern terms: is the psyche a substance or is it an epiphenomenon? In Aristotle's question is implied the idea that the psyche might represent a harmony or an attunement of various parts. If it is that, then it is not anything substantial in itself, it is just an epiphenomenon. Jung once illustrated what it means to think of the psyche as an epiphenomenon, saying that it is as though the brain were a bowl of hot spaghetti, and the psyche is the steam coming off of it.

This word "soul" is so fundamental to the work of analytical psychology that knowing its etymology is useful. In Homer, there are three main terms which may be translated as "soul" or "psyche": *psyche* is one, *thymos* is another, and *phren* or *phrenes* (plural) is a third. Roughly speaking, *psyche* referred to that which was thought of as the breath-soul, that which leaves the body with the breath when the body dies. The *thymos* was thought of as the blood-soul, the source of affect, of emotionality. The *phren* or *phrenes* refers to the midriff, the lungs or diaphragm. It is still enshrined in such words as "schizophrenic," for example. It refers to the location of the thymos, which was felt to be in the chest or diaphragm. The classical scholar Erwin Rohde writes:

> The belief in the existence of the psyche was the oldest and most primitive hypothesis adopted by mankind to explain the phenomena of dreams, swoons, and ecstatic visions; these mysterious states were accounted for by the intervention of a special material personality.[96]

For Homer there was a kind of double personality or second self; as Rohde describes it:

> For the most part the psyche is for him [Homer] and always remains a real "thing"—the man's second self. But that he had already begun to tread the slippery path in the course of which the psyche is transformed into an abstract "concept of life," is shown by the fact that he several times quite unmistakably uses the word "psyche" when we should say "life." [This tendency to abstraction was promoted

---

[96] *Psyche: The Cult of Souls in Ancient Greece*, p. 30.

by the development of] . . . the use of cremation . . . [and the general] tendency to turn the once material forces of man's inner life into abstractions.[97]

In Homer and in some of the philosophers' writings, what is now translated as magnanimous, which literally means great-souled, is expressed by such terms as *megalothymos* or *megalopsyche.* These earlier formulations, especially in Homer, had a much larger reference than our word magnanimous, which has the narrowed meaning of generosity. We need a term such as great-souled, but unfortunately there are no words to describe individual psyches of various sizes, although they vary tremendously in magnitude. The Greek word *megalothymos* might suffice.

Plato was the first to present an ordered, detailed theory of the psyche, and he divides the psyche, like the body politic described in the *Republic,* into three parts—the rational part, the spirited part and the appetitive part—or reason, will and appetite. This has certain similarities to modern formulations, to Freud's tripartite division of the psyche, for example, although not explicitly so.

According to Peters, the essence of Aristotle's definition of psyche is found in the following: "[The individual being is a] living or ensouled body composed of a material *(hyle)* and a formal *(eidos)* principle. The latter is the soul and . . . it may be defined as the first . . . *entelecheia* of an organic body."[98]

The scholar Renford Bambrough comments:

> The soul then must be a substance inasmuch as it is the form *[entelecheia]* of a natural body that potentially possesses life; and such substance is in fact realization, so that the soul is the realization of a body of this kind.[99]

Compared with the original Greek passage, one sees that Bambrough has interpreted the word *entelecheia* by reversing the word order of the sentence and by using both the word "form" and the word "realization" in characterizing the soul: ("The soul then must be a substance inasmuch as it is the *entelecheia* of a natural body . . .") That is doing what the alchemists did: defining the obscure in terms of the more obscure, but we have to go into these mysterious terminologies and particularly into the word *entelecheia* if we are to get any grasp of what this elusive subject of the psyche, which we discuss so glibly, really is.

Entelecheia is usually taken to mean realization or actuality, a condition in which a potentiality becomes an actuality, in keeping with its basic root in the

---

[97] Ibid., p. 31.

[98] *Greek Philosophical Terms*, pp. 172f.

[99] *The Philosophy of Aristotle*, p. 246.

word *telos,* meaning end, goal, or completion. However, we also have a modern word, entelechy, which has taken on an almost opposite meaning: the image of potential destiny residing latently in the germ or the beginnings of the organism. The image of an oak tree would be the entelechy of an acorn, for instance. The fact is that Aristotle does not clearly define the term *entelecheia.* His usage can be read in two ways. The word has *telos* at its root, which means that it points both to the goal of an organism as the goal exists in the seed and to the goal of the organism as it is realized in its full fulfillment; it has a uroboric quality. The Oxford English Dictionary defines *entelecheia* as "that which gives perfection to anything." Webster's Third International Unabridged Dictionary defines it as

> a supposititious [hypothetical] immanent but immaterial agency held by some Vitalists to regulate or direct the vital processes of an organism, especially toward the achievement of maturity.

To take this subject one step further, these concepts gave rise to the movement which was called Vitalism, defined as:

> The doctrine that phenomena of life possess a character *sui generis* by virtue of which they differ radically from physico-chemical phenomena. The vitalist ascribes the activities of living organisms to the operation of a "vital force" such as Driesch's "entelechy" or Bergson's *elan vital.* Opposed to Vitalism is biological mechanism which asserts that living phenomena can be explained exclusively in physico-chemical terms.[100]

Vitalism flourished through and up to the end of the nineteenth century. It has since been totally devalued by orthodox science and one might say has become heresy. It would be impossible now to get a paper that contains any hint of Vitalism published in a scientific journal. Jung was familiar with the Vitalism of his time and with Hans Driesch in particular. It is not that he was influenced by the Vitalists but that he recognized the fact that some of the Vitalist ideas paralleled some of his own empirical discoveries.

Not much on Vitalism is available now, but the Jungian analyst Marilyn Nagy, in her book on philosophical issues, has a section on the school and on Driesch:

> Hans Driesch [whose dates were 1867 to 1941] began his career as a student of zoology . . . and finally received his doctorate in biology. . . .
> He was at first completely committed to the mechanistic principle of his famous teacher [Enheckle]. But while he was experimenting with the eggs of sea ur-

---

[100] Dagobert D. Runes, ed., *Dictionary of Philosophy,* p. 133.

chins he discovered something which startlingly contradicted the prevalent theory of morphogenetic development. If the fertilized ovum is divided at the stage of the first two or four blastomeres, then two or four complete organisms, though smaller in size than a normal size sea urchin, can be reared from those divided cells. . . . The conclusions he drew as a result of his experimental work led him far from the laboratory, into the field of philosophy where he finally made his career. [He took] a professorship at Heidelberg in [philosophy. His idea is that] inorganic nature follows the mechanistic laws of nature. In the case of organic nature, however, we must postulate a *non-material ordering entity* to account for the fact of life and for the goal-directed patterning which we see in life. . . .

In honor of what he had learned from his reading of Aristotle, Driesch named his non-material agent "entelechy." [He called it a kind of whole-making causality, and wrote:]

"There is something in the organism's behavior—in the widest sense of the word—which is opposed to an inorganic resolution of the same and which shows that the living organism is more than a sum or an aggregate of its parts, that it is insufficient to call the organism a 'typically combined body' without further explanation. This something we call entelechy. . . . [which] is a factor of nature, though it only relates to nature in space. . . . Entelechy's role in spatial nature may be formulated both mechanically and energetically. Introspective analysis shows that human reason possesses a special kind of category—individuality—by the aid of which it is able to understand to its own satisfaction what entelechy is; the category of individuality thus completing the concept of ideal nature in a positive way."[101]

Here, Driesch is starting to take the data of psychology and relate them to the data of biology, which in orthodox scientific procedure would now be impermissible. He concludes that introspective analysis shows that human reason possesses a special kind of category—individuality. Thus one can recognize what entelechy is by one's own subjective psychic experience.

Jung refers to the term "entelechy" in the Vitalist sense. Here we see the flowering of Aristotle's concept of *entelecheia.* Jung says,

The goal of the individuation process is the synthesis of the self. From another point of view the term "entelechy" might be preferable to "synthesis." There is an empirical reason why "entelechy" is, in certain conditions, more fitting: the symbols of wholeness frequently occur at the beginning of the individuation process, indeed they can often be observed in the first dreams of early infancy. This observation says much for the *a priori* existence of potential wholeness, and on this account the idea of *entelechy* instantly recommends itself. But in so far as the individuation process occurs, empirically speaking, as a synthesis, it looks, para-

---

[101] *Philosophical Issues in the Psychology of C.G. Jung*, pp. 247ff

doxically enough, as if something already existent were being put together. From this point of view, the term "synthesis" is also applicable.[102]

Another major term in Aristotle is *hyle,* which means matter. Aristotle originated this usage; he was the first to establish in a clear, conceptual way the idea of matter, as distinguished from form *(eidos),* so that he speaks of the twin entities form and matter, *eidos* and *hyle.* Eduard Zeller comments:

> All change presupposes an unchangeable and ever-becoming something that has not become; . . . its nature is twofold. The substrate, which becomes something and upon which the change takes place; and the qualities in the communications of which to the substrate this change consists. Aristotle used the word matter in a new sense to denote his substrate.[103]

Form, which was an incorporeal entity and therefore of a spiritlike nature, was thought to imprint itself on matter and create a specific object. Matter without that addition of form is what Aristotle thought of as first matter, which is undefined and unlimited, the common substrate of everything and without any particular qualities at all. It has to have a form imposed on it in order to become something definite. Psychologically, form and matter relate to archetype and ego. In that regard, Jung remarks: "Matter represents the *concreteness* of God's thoughts and is, therefore, the very thing that makes individuation possible, with all its consequences."[104]

The idea that matter is the source of individuation is originally Aristotelian. Matter is what makes individual objects manifest. Jung, of course, is applying that idea to the concreteness of individual ego existence, that which gives material reality to archetypal forms. As an example, a modern dream illustrates the psychological relationship of the terms form and matter:

> I am sitting before an ancient intaglio of a crucifixion. It is metal but it is partially covered with a waxlike substance which leads me to discover that there are candles above it, one on each side, and I realize I am to light these, and make the wax run down into the intaglio and that this has something to do with the ritual-like meal I am about to eat. I light the candles and the wax does run down into the empty form of the crucifixion. When it is full I take it down from the wall above me and am at my meal.

---

[102] "The Psychology of the Child Archetype," *The Archetypes and the Collective Unconscious,* CW 9i, par. 278; see also CW 11, par. 960; CW 12, par. 248; CW 9ii, par. 282.
[103] *Outlines of the History of Greek Philosophy,* p. 193.
[104] "A Psychological Approach to the Dogma of the Trinity," *Psychology and Religion,* CW 11, par. 252.

The dreamer then begins to have some worries about whether he can digest the meal or not. But the basic image is that molten candle wax flows down into this mold, where it solidifies into the image of the crucifixion, so there is the idea of indefinite matter, represented by the melted wax on the one hand, and on the other hand, form, which is empty and does not exist as a real entity until it is filled with the wax, which it then molds into a copy of itself.

This dream is an unusual example, arising in the life of a person who experienced extreme deprivation in childhood, and in whom ego development was taking place in the late twenties, although such ego development ordinarily occurs in the first decade of life. It is a picture of what Jung speaks of as the Self as a prefiguration of the ego. The man was a Catholic, so this kind of imagery was immediately available to him. The intaglio would be an image of the Self which undifferentiated ego-stuff is pouring itself into. It then has to be assimilated—eaten, taken in. This dream shows the Aristotelian images alive and functioning in the modern psyche.

This same duality of form and matter is found in the additional Aristotelian terms of "the mover" and "the moved." The moved corresponds to the condition of matter. As Aristotle understood it, matter is inert in itself, requiring some dynamic from outside itself to move it along. Form supplies that dynamic. Where form and matter come into contact motion always arises, and the ultimate cause of this motion can only lie in something which is itself unmoved. That is Aristotle's position. Psychologically, the moved corresponds to the ego, and what one sees doing the moving is what we call emotion, the carrier of libido. The source of that emotion, to the extent that one finds it unmoved, would correspond to the static Self. Obviously, even though Aristotle was very much occupied with ego-consciousness, a great deal of basic psychological material and imagery crept into his thinking.

We find it also in his concept of the four causes, the so-called *aitia.* Every entity in existence, according to Aristotle, has four bases, four *aitia* for its existence. We see here that the quaternity as an ordering principle is imposing itself on his thinking in the same way that it did for Empedocles, who said that all of reality is based on four elements. The four causes, according to Aristotle, are these: the material cause, the formal cause, the moving or efficient cause, and the final cause. Aristotle's example is this:

Suppose that we have a bronze statue of a deity. The material cause of that statue is bronze, what the statue is made of; that is a rather loose use of the word "cause" as we think of it, but the word had a looser meaning then. One of the bases of the statue's existence is the material it is made out of, bronze. Its formal cause is the image to be created, which is in the mind of the sculptor. There are probably other images of Zeus, shall we say, so he already had the image in his mind as to what Zeus looked like, and that image, which in itself is incorporeal, is the formal cause. The moving or the efficient cause is the sculptor who does the work, who makes the mold and pours the bronze, and the final cause is the purpose for the whole operation, which we'll say is to adorn a temple to Zeus, and therefore the final cause is the worship of the god.

There are psychological parallels to those four causes. Roughly speaking, we can say that sensation tells us that something exists, that it is a fact, that it is there. This would correspond to the material cause. Thinking tells us what it is, what category it belongs to. Is it a house? Is it a table, a chair? That would be the formal cause, determined by thinking. Feeling tells us whether we like it or not, so it is not exactly the moving cause, but it certainly determines whether that thing is going to move toward us or away from us. Finally, intuition tells us where it comes from and where it is going, so it has some parallel to Aristotle's final cause. These are not precise equivalences; the quaternity operates in different contexts in analogous but not identical ways.

The four causes of a dream can be outlined in the same way. The material cause of a dream in most cases can be seen to be the personal life events that have immediately preceded the dream. That is very often the case, at least, and the dream imagery is an allusion to those personal life events. The formal cause of the dream will be the archetypal imagery that is expressed in it. The moving or efficient cause of the dream we postulate to be the dynamic aspect of the Self. The final cause of the dream would be the dream's purpose, which we discover when we find its meaning. Its purpose may seem to be compensation of a one-sided conscious attitude or, more generally, an increase in consciousness. In this way, four causes can be applied in a general sort of way to dreams, too.

Another concept from Aristotle is the term *meson*. The word means "the mean." In his essay on ethics, Aristotle asks, what is virtue?, and answers, the mean between two opposites. The scholar Renford Bambrough elaborates:

> Virtue, then, is a disposition involving choice. It consists in a mean, relative to us, defined by reason and as the reasonable man would define it. It is a mean between two vices—one of excess, the other of deficiency. . . . [As an example, he says:] As for honor and dishonor, the mean is *[megalopsychos]* grandeur of soul whereas the excess is a sort of vanity, and the deficiency meanness of soul.[105]

---

[105] *The Philosophy of Aristotle*, pp. 309ff.

This particular example corresponds to the psychological opposites of inflation on the one hand and what can be called negative inflation on the other. The mean would be the proper balance in which the ego recognizes its limits and is neither inflated grandly nor deflated into guilty insignificance.

Behind this conception of the mean is the image of the balance of Themis. That balance later became the scales held by the figure of Justice. But what is most interesting about this conception of the mean—not altogether persuasive as a definition of virtue—is what seems to be going on in Aristotle's mind as he has it. Aristotle is the real formulator of modern logic, the one who established the law of the excluded middle. This refers to the fact that Aristotelian logic does not permit a third *(tertium non datur,* the third is not given). According to Aristotelian logic, either a statement is true or it is not true. Either A is B or A is not B. No third alternative is possible in the world of logic, but here in the case of the mean, Aristotle is sneaking in a third between the opposites.

The development of logic was absolutely necessary for the historical function Aristotle was serving, because he was expanding ego-consciousness, whose chief operation is to discriminate and split things into opposites. That is what consciousness does. However, this Aristotelian logic is still the bane of the depth psychologist's existence, and Jung addresses this issue in the very first page of "Answer to Job," which he begins with his "Lectori Benevolo," his "To the Kind Reader." In this note, he says that he is going to talk about things that Aristotelian logic cannot be applied to:

> In what follows, I shall speak of the venerable objects of religious belief. Whoever talks of such matters inevitably runs the risk of being torn to pieces by the two parties who are in mortal conflict about those very things. This conflict is due to the strange supposition that a thing is true only if it presents itself as a *physical* fact. Thus some people believe it to be physically true that Christ was born as the son of a virgin, while others deny this as a physical impossibility. Everyone can see that there is no logical solution to this conflict and that one would do better not to get involved in such sterile disputes. Both are right and both are wrong. Yet they could easily reach agreement if only they dropped the word "physical." "Physical" is not the only criterion of truth: there are also *psychic* truths.[106]

In this passage, Jung tries to challenge Aristotelian logic, which is actually a mode of functioning, one could say, of simple-minded people. It is a great discovery when one first makes it, but it is gravely limited so far as the phenomena of depth psychology are concerned.

---

[106] *Psychology and Religion,* CW 11, par. 553.

A final Aristotelean concept involves the term encountered earlier with Empedocles, the term *katharsis*. In his essay on poetics, Aristotle describes tragedy as the "imitation of a serious and complete action. . . . By means of pity and fear it contrives to purify *[katharsis]* the emotions of pity and fear."[107] This *katharsis* corresponds approximately to what we speak of in psychology as abreaction, in which an unconscious complex is drained or vented, though not necessarily assimilated. It is drained at least, and the pressure of it is relieved for a while, like an abscess that is drained but is not healed by the drainage and will gradually fill up again. That is parallel to what abreaction does for the complex.

Jung remarks about this matter in relationship to the drama, in *Symbols of Transformation,* speaking of the function of the theater: "One might describe the theater, somewhat unaesthetically, as an institution for working out private complexes in public."[108] That is a variation of the Aristotelian notion of catharsis. In a theatrical presentation, what we react to is that which is relevant to our psychology, that which we identify with, and different people with different psychologies have quite different reactions to a given play. The whole mirroring effect of the theater and how it can bring into awareness the archetypal dimension of the psyche is a subject still awaiting psychological exploration.

---

[107] *Poetics,* 1449b., quoted in Bambrough, *The Philosophy of Aristotle,* p. 416.
[108] CW 5, par. 48.

9
Zeno of Citium

Zeno of Citium (not to be confused with Zeno of Elea) is the father of the famous school of Stoicism, which was named after the *stoa,* the porch on which the discourse was initially held. He is the first of a trio of Stoics: Zeno, Cleanthes and Chrisippus, who covered three successive generations, each taught by the previous one. Their doctrines are so intermixed that we cannot separate them; what can be said about Zeno applies to Stoicism in general.

Zeno lived from approximately 340 to 265 B.C. He was born in Citium, Cypress, of Phoenician-Semitic ancestry. Several scholars have remarked that Zeno introduced into the rationalistic stream of Greek philosophy a current of Semitic religiosity that brought to Stoicism a more religious flavor than was seen in some of the other schools. He fathered a quite profound philosophical religion, which later included among its major authors even a Roman emperor, Marcus Aurelius. Stoicism subsequently became the major world view of the most prominent Roman statesmen, and, for a time, of the Roman empire in general.

Two categories of Stoic doctrine are of interest psychologically. The first deals with the nature of the universe, and the second with ethics, the way human beings should live their daily lives. Stoicism was the first philosophical school to give such great emphasis to standards of human behavior.

According to the Stoics the basic principle of the universe was the *logos.* It was commonly spoken of as the *logos spermatikos,* usually translated as "seminal reason." This refers to the divine word that is cast like a seed into matter.

Diogenes Laertius, a compiler of Greek philosophy in the second century A.D., describes this aspect of Stoicism:

> God is one and the same with Reason, Fate, and Zeus. . . . In the beginning he was by himself; he transformed the whole of substance through air into water, and just as in animal generation the seed has a moist vehicle, so in cosmic moisture God, who is the seminal reason of the universe *[logos spermatikos],* remains behind in the moisture . . . adapting matter to himself with a view to the next stage of creation. Thereupon he created first of all the four elements, fire, water, air and earth. . . . The four elements together constitute unqualified substance or matter. Fire is the hot element, water the moist, air the cold, earth the dry. . . . Fire has the uppermost place; it is also called aether, and in it the sphere of the fixed stars is first created; [so here there is an image of the uppermost circle of the cosmos as a ring or sphere of fire] then comes the sphere of the planets, next to that the air, then the water,

and lowest of all the earth, which is at the centre of all.

The world in their view is ordered by reason and providence [by *nous* and *pro-noia*. In this case, *nous* is a synonym for *logos,* here translated as reason, which is also a common translation of *logos*]—inasmuch as reason pervades every part of it, just as does the soul in us. Only there is a difference of degree; in some parts there is more of it, in others less. For through some parts it passes as a "hold" or containing force . . . while through others it passes as intelligence, as in the ruling part of the soul. Thus, then, the whole world is a living being, endowed with soul and reason, and having aether [or fire] for its ruling principle. [Here, fire and *logos* are equivalent.][109]

It is useful to contemplate this profound and basic image, which appears in various traditional world views and also in modern dreams. The image is of a fiery world soul that surrounds the known universe, penetrates the material world and governs through this penetration. It sends off sparks of itself which generate replicas of the world soul in individual human beings. The essence of the individual soul is of the same substance as the world soul; it is one of those sparks, those *logos* seeds generated by the divine fire that contains and pervades the universe. Peters characterizes *logos* as follows:

> The *logos* considered as a unified entity contains within itself, on the analogy of animal sperm, the growth powers of exemplars of all the individuals. These individual *logoi* are imperishable.[110]

This image may be found in some of the most unusual places. For instance, it appears in the parables of Christ. Mark 4:3-14 describes in parable the nature of the kingdom of Heaven:

> Hearken; Behold, there went out a sower to sow: And it came to pass, as he sowed, some [of the seeds] fell by the way side, and the fowls of the air came and devoured it up. And some fell on stony ground, where it had not much earth; and immediately it sprang up, because it had no depth of earth: But when the sun was up, it was scorched; and because it had no root, it withered away. And some fell among thorns, and the thorns grew up, and choked it, and it yielded no fruit. And other fell on good ground, and did yield fruit that sprang up and increased; . . . [He then explains the parable:] The sower soweth the word *[logos].*[111]

This is a pure Stoic image. It may be an original archetypal image that emerged spontaneously from the unconscious or it may have been picked up

---

[109] In R.D. Hicks, *Lives of the Eminent Philosophers,* VII, 136-139, vol. 2, pp. 241ff.

[110] *Greek Philosophical Terms*, p. 110.

[111] Authorized King James Version.

from another source, but it is the same basic idea: the heavenly fire sows sparks of itself to generate what we can now understand psychologically as the potentiality of consciousness in individuals.

This whole image of light descending into matter became prominent in Gnosticism and in the Kabala of Isaac Luria, where it appears as the image of the divine light being poured into vessels which could not hold it, so that it spattered out into matter in a shower of sparks.

The same image may be found in alchemy as the *scintilla.* Jung discusses it at considerable length in *Mysterium Coniunctionis:*

> In Khunrath the scintilla is the same as the elixir: "Now the elixir is well and truly called a shining splendour or perfect scintilla [spark] of him who alone is the Mighty and Strong. . . . It is the true Aqua Permanens, eternally living." The "radical moisture" is "animated . . . by a fiery spark of the World-Soul, for the spirit of the Lord filleth the whole world." He also speaks of a plurality of sparks: "There are . . . fiery sparks of the World-Soul, that is of the light of nature, dispersed or scattered at God's command in and through the fabric of the great world into all fruits of the elements everywhere." . . . The Son of the Great World . . . is filled . . . with a fiery spark of Ruach Elohim, the spirit, breath, wind or blowing of the triune God, from . . . the Body, Spirit, and Soul of the World.[112]

The image is an amalgamation of a Jewish concept, the Ruach Elohim (the Spirit of God); the Christian Trinity (the triune God); and the soul or body of the world from Stoicism. Jung furthermore adds a note from Greek mythology: "This is beyond doubt Proteus, the seed god." In Jung's passage, all are interconnected, a kind of prelude to psychological amplification.

Another feature of the Stoic universe is that it is governed throughout by *pronoia,* which is almost always translated as "providence" and means, literally, "foreseeing." It can also, by extension, mean "forethought." In general usage it also means "taking care of," which is denoted in our use of the term, "providential." In one place it is described this way:

> In Stoic philosophy, . . . *[pronoia]* became an important concept for describing the emanation of the purposeful operations of a world-force possessing divine status and working for the benefit of mankind as well as the perfection of nature. *Pronoia,* providence, thus gained a religious significance and became an expression of religious piety. In fact, among the Stoics, it was raised to the level of an indisputable dogma. Chance is ruled out, because everything runs its course according to an implanted divine law of development which is itself divine.[113]

---

[112] CW 14, par. 50.

[113] *New International Dictionary of New Testament Theology,* vol. 1, p. 694.

This *pronoia,* this providence, is one of the qualities of the fiery logos that permeates the world. The concept of *pronoia* has received very widespread usage and adaptation. Thomas Aquinas has a chapter on divine providence in his *Summa.* He says,

> We must say, however, that all things are subject to divine providence, not only in general, but even in their own individual being. This is made evident thus. For since every agent acts for an end, the ordering of effects toward that end extends as far as the causality of the first agent extends. Whence it happens that in the effects of an agent something takes place which has no reference towards the end, because the effect comes from some other cause outside the intention of the agent. But the causality of God, Who is the first agent, extends to all beings not only as to the constituent principles of species, but also as to the individualizing principles; not only of things incorruptible, but also of things corruptible. Hence all things that exist in whatsoever manner are necessarily directed by God towards the end.[114]

This divine providence is a legacy of the Stoic idea that the divine spark that motivates individuals derives from the divine fire. It is a little piece of the divine soul and therefore it carries out the transpersonal intention of the divine fire that it came from. This is a totally teleological image: the universe, its operation and everything that goes on in it are purposeful and therefore have meaning.

From the point of view of empirical psychology, on one level we can understand this doctrine to be a projection onto the outer world of the teleological pattern and purpose that reside in the Self. There is evidence from analytic work that the Self, as the center of the unconscious, has a purposeful guiding and directive function in relation to the ego, once the ego is in relation to it. It is equivalent to providence. That relationship could be called latent providence, because it does not usually manifest in a clear and fruitful way until it has come into consciousness.

A second level is the question of whether something equivalent to divine providence operates in the larger world or, in other words, beyond the psychology of the individual. There are hints that it may, in the experience of synchronicity, where apparently meaningful connections between individual circumstances and external events seem to carry a kind of revelatory quality. It is possible to say that something like divine providence or transpersonal meaningfulness does indeed intersect at times with the personal life of the ego. Unlike the Stoics, however, we cannot claim that this occurs constantly and uniformly. Such an assumption could only be an act of faith. Jung remarks on this subject:

---

[114] *Basic Writings of St. Thomas Aquinas,* vol. 1, p. 232.

The world into which we are born is brutal and cruel, and at the same time of divine beauty. Which element we think outweighs the other, whether meaninglessness or meaning, is a matter of temperament. [One can take "meaning" to be approximately equivalent to providence]. If meaninglessness were absolutely preponderant, the meaningfulness of life would vanish to an increasing degree with each step in our development. But that is—or seems to me—not the case. Probably, as in all metaphysical questions, both are true: Life is—or has—meaning and meaninglessness. I cherish the anxious hope that meaning will preponderate and win the battle.[115]

One cannot be too dogmatic on things as uncertain and borderline as these questions, but it is possible to gather evidence to support the thought that providence does indeed exist as a transpersonal force in the collective psyche. In other words, it is found not just in the individual psyche, but in the collective psyche to which we are all connected through the collective unconscious, and which is also connected to physical reality as we know by the phenomenon of synchronicity. There is evidence that such an entity as providence exists, but it is latent and not apparent in any consistent or reliable way. It comes into realization when an individual conscious ego touches it. In other words, human consciousness, by seeking diligently for the latent providential meaning in a given personal experience, creates that providential meaning as it discovers it. The cooperation of an individual ego is required for it to shift from a latent to an overt condition.

This formulation is just a variation of Jung's notion of the unconscious or dimly conscious God-image that needs contact with the conscious ego in order to bring it into full realization. These matters are well worth reflecting on; when one does reflect on them, one is dealing with an image that has gripped humanity since the dawn of rational thinking, as evidenced in the fact that it goes back to the Stoics.

A second major category of Stoic doctrine deals with ethics and human behavior. One of the terms that apply to Stoic ethics is *apatheia*. That is the original version of our word "apathy," but for the Stoics it had a somewhat different connotation. Literally it means "without pathos," "without affect" or "without emotion or suffering." The goal of the Stoic wise man was to achieve *apatheia*.

Peters comments that *apatheia* had no place in Aristotle. For Aristotle the goal was the mean, a mean between extreme *pathe* of one kind or another. For the Epicureans, the Hedonists, the goal was to choose one pathos, the pleasure

---

[115] *Memories, Dreams, Reflections*, pp. 358f.

pathos, and rule out the opposite, the pain pathos. But, says Peters:

> The radical point of difference between Epicurus and the Stoics in this regard is the latter's insistence that *all* the *pathe* are irrational movements against nature, at least as defined by Zeno. . . . Thus it would seem that the Stoic is concerned with eradicating the *pathe,* the Peripatetic [the Aristotelian] with moderating them [finding the mean between them], and the Epicurean with discriminating between the good and evil among them.[116]

These differences have a direct psychological relevance. Psychological analysis does promote something akin to *apatheia,* because it deliberately makes the effort to promote disidentification from the affects. Certainly the goal is not to remove the affects—that would be an act of dissociative repression—but rather to objectify them. This can only be done when the ego is not identified with the affects; when they are objectified, one recognizes that the affects come from the Self and not from the ego, and they then are experienced as manifestations of transpersonal libido. This takes the Stoic goal of *apatheia* one step further than the Stoic's position, which ran into the criticism that it was promoting human insensitivity.

If we look back on the Stoics in historical and psychological terms, we see that one of Stoicism's major functions was the strengthening and disciplining of the ego. Thus, it held that salvation for all the pains and sufferings of the world can be achieved if the ego takes the right attitude towards things. In other words, Stoicism assumed a degree of ego potency that the ego does not really have, but that is the kind of thing that the young of all ages characteristically do. One has to exaggerate the importance of the ego in order to build it up, so that it can start taking responsibility for itself.

Another of the goals of the Stoic wise man was *autarcheia,* which is usually translated "self-sufficiency," but more literally would be "self-rule." In achieving the Stoic virtue of *apatheia* there was a recognition that no harm could befall one from an affective state that one did not allow to exist. This resulted in the generation within the individual of *autarcheia,* self-sufficiency, that was the essence of virtue itself and required no other life fulfillment in order for one to be happy and contented. The Stoics are surely the original authors of the axiom that virtue is its own reward, which we can recognize psychologically on another level: consciousness is its own reward; it brings a satisfaction that nothing can compare with.

---

[116] *Greek Philosophical Terms,* p. 19.

Autarcheia as a quality of virtue becomes a commonplace in both Stoicism and in later Platonic tradition in Plotinus, who refines this issue further. Living several centuries later, he was at a different stage of psychological development, and he applied the idea of aut*arche*ia to the One, the primordial source, his elemental God-image, rather than to the ego. The Stoics did not make that distinction, so that they attributed certain qualities of the Self to the ego, which in modern terms would be a dubious operation. The ego is by no means self-sufficient, but the Self is, and to the extent that the ego has a living conscious connection to the Self, it shares somewhat in its *autarcheia* and can experience it to some degree. If it identifies with the *autarcheia* of the Self, however, it is in for a fall. The psyche corrects such one-sidedness.

Erich Neumann uses the term "autarchy" in his description of early ego development. He writes:

> We shall have to concern ourselves with the problem of autarchy at all stages of our inquiry, because it is bound up with an important trend in man's development, namely with the problem of his self-formation. . . .
> Autarchy is just as necessary a goal of life and development as is adaptation. Self-development, self-differentiation, and self-formation are trends of the libido no less legitimate than the extraverted relation to the object and the introverted relation to the subject. The negative evaluation implied by the terms "autoeroticism," "autism," and "narcissism" is only justified in pathological cases. . . . In many cases, therefore, the appearance of uroboric symbolism [which he considers to be an image of self-sufficiency, of autarchy], especially if its formative and stabilizing character is strongly marked, as, for instance, in the mandala, indicates that the ego is moving toward the self, rather than in the direction of objective adaptation.[117]

Neumann makes the important point that psychological experience and development move between the poles of adaptation to external objective reality on the one hand and autarchy on the other hand. The introvert will spend more time at the autarchic pole of that continuum, and the extravert will be more toward the external adaptation pole.

The scholar Edwyn Bevan offers a good summary of Stoic doctrine:

> [The Stoics considered that] human life was a chaos, in which blind Desire was the propelling force, and action was spasmodic, furious, vain—a misery of craving for ever disappointed and for ever renewed. This blind Desire was the other great constituent, besides the Fear, in that human misery which the gospel of Zeno claimed to meet. . . . If Zeno was able to put man in possession of a good, secure from all

---

[117] *The Origins and History of Consciousness,* pp. 34f.

chances of the morrow, then the desire of man need be directed to nothing beyond it. There was no place for either Desire or Fear any more.

It was such a good which Stoicism bade men see within their reach. Zeno asked in effect what happiness really was, and he found it—this is the essential point—not in a particular sort of sensation or sum of sensations . . . but in an attitude of the Will. [The ego will; there is the emphasis on the ego.] A man is happy when what he wills exists. . . . I am happy when I do not want things to be any other than they are.[118]

Why should I adjust my will to what happens? Why should I refuse to consider any pain that comes to me an evil? The Stoic had an answer ready: Because everything that happens is determined by the sovereign Reason [in other words, by *pronoia*]. If you discard the Stoic belief in the Rational Purpose controlling the course of the world . . . [then you are not able any longer to] call everything that happens to you good.[119]

Zeno taught that God is Body, [matter] but it was not dead stuff which constituted the world. The thing which Zeno was concerned above all others to affirm was that this stuff was actually Reason *[logos]*. The Universe is a living being; that was the fundamental formula of Stoic Physics. Nothing could be farther from what is understood by Materialism in modern times.[120]

He explained that God in His proper being, in the state which realized all His potentiality, was not the whole of matter but the finest part of it. He described this part, following Heraclitus, as a fire, or as a fiery ether, more subtle than the common air and fire we know. This fiery ether was identical with pure Reason. Somehow part of the fire had got condensed and heavy and lost its divinity. . . . Part, however, of the original fiery ether retained its proper form, and this constituted the active power in the Universe, whilst the rest was the passive material upon which it acted. All round the world was an envelope of the fiery ether, pure and unmixed, but it also penetrated the whole mass, as its soul. The orderly working of Nature was its operation: organic beings grew according to regular types, because the Divine Reason was in them as a *logos spermatikos,* a *formula* of life developing from a germ. Even upon earth some of the divine fire retained its pure essence—the reasonable souls, each one a particle of fiery ether, which dwelt in the hearts of men.[121]

[So men were bade to] surrender their wills. Every movement in the world was as much the expression of a Supreme Purpose as the voluntary movements of an animal were of its individual purpose. Chance had no place in the close-knit process

[118] *Stoics and Sceptics*, p. 28.

[119] Ibid., p. 30.

[120] Ibid., p. 42.

[121] Ibid., p. 43.

which might be called Fate or Destiny *[heimarmene]*, but which was really Intelligent Law and all-pervading Providence *[pronoia]*. It was for the faith in Providence above all else that the Stoic stood in the ancient world.[122]

Jung invokes Stoicism prominently in the last chapter of *Mysterium Coniunctionis,* in which he talks about the three stages of the *coniunctio.* The first stage of the *coniunctio* actually is a *separatio.* It is expressed by a separation of a pair of opposites, thought of as either mind and body or soul and body. The central idea is that mind and body or spirit and matter if you will, have to undergo separation from their original state of mutual contamination before they can undergo a union, a conscious *coniunctio.* This purification by *separatio* can be expressed symbolically as a death, a *mortificatio,* or as a separation of the head from the body, a decapitation. Jung says about that particular symbolism:

> In order to bring about their subsequent reunion [the reunion of mind and body or spirit and matter], the mind must be separated from the body—which is equivalent to "voluntary death"—for only separated things can unite. . . . Dorn obviously meant a discrimination and dissolution of the "composite" [the contaminated mixture], the composite state being one in which the affectivity of the body has a disturbing influence on the rationality of the mind. The aim of this separation was to free the mind from the influence of the "bodily appetites and the heart's affections," and to establish a spiritual position which is supraordinate to the turbulent sphere of the body. This leads at first to a dissociation of the personality and a violation of the merely natural man.
>
> This preliminary step, in itself a clear blend of Stoic philosophy and Christian psychology, is indispensable for the differentiation of consciousness. Modern psychotherapy makes use of the same procedure when it objectifies the affects and instincts and confronts consciousness with them. But the separation of the spiritual and vital spheres, and the subordination of the latter to the rational standpoint, is not satisfactory inasmuch as reason alone cannot do complete or even adequate justice to the irrational facts of the unconscious. In the long run it does not pay to cripple life by insisting on the primacy of the spirit. . . . A permanent and uncomplicated state of spiritualization is therefore such a rarity that its possessors are canonized by the Church.[123]

This procedure is the first stage of the *coniunctio,* and it is an important feature of the analytic process, because until that stage has been reached, there can be no question of a greater integration. In other words, one has to go through a Stoic phase of individuation.

---

[122] Ibid., pp. 43f.
[123] CW 14, par. 671f.

We have almost no fragments of the writings of the original Stoics, but wonderfully, something has been saved from Cleanthes, the student of Zeno the founder of Stoicism. "The Hymn of Cleanthes" has come down to us, a statement by an authentic original Stoic philosopher:

O God most glorious, called by many a name,
Nature's great King, through endless years the same;
Omnipotence, who by thy just decree
Controllest all, hail, Zeus, for unto thee
Behoves thy creatures in all lands to call.
We are thy children, we alone, of all
On earth's broad ways that wander to and fro,
Bearing thine image wheresoe'er we go.
Wherefore with songs of praise thy power I
    will forth shew.
Lo! yonder heaven, that round the earth is wheeled,
Follows thy guidance, still to thee doth yield
Glad homage; thine unconquerable hand
Such flaming minister the [firebrand]
Wieldeth, a sword two-edged, whose deathless might
Pulsates through all that Nature brings to light;
Vehicle of the universal Word, that flows
Through all, and in the light celestial glows
Of stars both great and small. O King of Kings
Through ceaseless ages, God, whose purpose brings
To birth, whate'er on land or in the sea
Is wrought, or in high heaven's immensity;
Save what the sinner works infatuate.
Nay, but thou knowest to make crooked straight:
Chaos to thee is order: in thine eyes
The unloved is lovely, who did'st harmonize
Things evil with things good, that there should be
One Word through all things everlastingly.
One Word—whose voice alas! the wicked spurn;
Insatiate for the good their spirits yearn:
Yet seeing see not, neither hearing hear
God's universal law, which those revere,
By reason guided, happiness who win.
The rest, unreasoning, diverse shapes of sin
Self-prompted follow: for an idle name
Vainly they wrestle in the lists of fame:
Others inordinately Riches woo,
Or dissolute, the joys of flesh pursue,
Now here, now there they wander, fruitless still,

For ever seeking good and finding ill.
Zeus the all-bountiful, whom darkness shrouds,
Whose lightning lightens in the thunder clouds;
Thy children save from error's deadly sway:
Turn thou the darkness from their souls away:
Vouchsafe that unto knowledge they attain;
For thou by knowledge art made strong to reign
O'er all, and all things ruleth righteously.
So by thee honored, we will honor thee,
Praising thy works continually with songs,
As mortals should; nor higher meed belongs
E'en to the gods, than justly to adore
The universal law forever more. [124]

---

[124] Trans. James Adam, in R.D. Hicks, *Stoic and Epicurean*, pp. 14f.

10
Philo

In the three centuries which elapsed between Zeno of Citium and Philo, the nature of the psyche changed significantly and the change may be seen in Philo. His importance has been relatively overlooked, as E.R. Goodenough notes in his remarks on the book jacket of his *Introduction to Philo Judaeus:*

> It is amusing to speculate on the fury which would have arisen in scholarly circles had the works of Philo been newly discovered instead of the Qumran scrolls. For Philo was an exact contemporary of Jesus and Paul in Alexandria, where he was one of the leading Jews of the city, and from him we have the equivalent of twelve volumes in the Loeb Series, all interpreting Judaism. Yet most Jews and Gentiles alike have tacitly united in ignoring him, or in dismissing him at second or third hand. Such neglect of so strategic a figure has no parallel.

Philo lived from approximately 25 B.C. to 45 A.D. He was born in Alexandria and spent all his life there, a member of an immensely wealthy and influential family belonging to the large Jewish community. Goodenough compares his family to the Rothschilds in nineteenth-century England. He was a devout Jew, profoundly versed in the Hebrew scriptures. At the same time, he was completely at home in Greek philosophy, and he set himself the task of combining and reconciling these two very diverse traditions.

Philo is a neglected and unappreciated figure of great magnitude for cultural history; he suffered the fate of individuals who transcend factional differences. He has been ignored or disparaged by the Hebrew literal religionists on the one hand, and by the Greek rationalists on the other, because he transcended each of them. His work is important for depth psychology as an early example of the translation of psychic realities from a concrete religious context into another framework, in order to make them viable for a new age. That is the task confronting Jungian psychology today.

He called his method *allegoria,* perceiving that the principles and concepts of Greek philosophy were expressed allegorically in the Hebrew Bible, especially in the five books of Moses. Goodenough says that Philo's central idea is

> that the deeper content of Judaism was a revelation of the concepts of Platonic and Pythagorean philosophy, Stoic and Platonic ethics, and of the way to reach the reality behind those conceptions in mystic ascent. . . . The two traditions of thought, the Jewish and the Greek, so completely blended in his mind that the favorite dis-

pute as to whether he was more Greek or more Jewish has little meaning. Out of the two strands he had woven himself a single cloth, warp and woof. He read Plato in terms of Moses and Moses in terms of Plato, to the point that he was convinced that each had said essentially the same things. Indeed, he used to say that Plato had cribbed his ideas from Moses, but his biblical interpretations often read as though he thought Moses had been trained by Plato. [By "Moses," Goodenough means the Pentateuch, the first five books, because Moses was generally credited as their author.] Philo, an open-minded Jew, no more rejected the best of the Gentile world than the modern American Jew should be expected to reject Einstein or Shakespeare. He not only remained loyal to Jewish people and customs, but he made a herculean effort to see meaning in the Jewish traditions in such terms of 'meaning' as the deepest and most valuable knowledge of his day had taught him.[125]

Philo was no dry, abstract scholar. He had a profound inner life; he had experienced the living reality of the concepts that he wrote about. His was an unusual combination of an introverted and an extraverted life. His very extensive writings indicate the power of profound introversion, but he was also actively engaged in political affairs. Late in his life, for instance, he headed a Jewish delegation to the Emperor Caligula in Rome to protest persecution of the Jewish community of Alexandria.

Philo makes some very revealing comments about himself in one of his treatises, suggesting that he was essentially a modern man:

There was once a time when by devoting myself to philosophy and to contemplation of the world and its parts I achieved the enjoyment of that Mind which is truly beautiful, desirable, and blessed; for I lived in constant communion with sacred utterances and teachings, in which I greedily and insatiably rejoiced. No base or worldly thoughts occurred to me, nor did I grovel for glory, wealth, or bodily comfort, but I seemed ever to be borne aloft in the heights in a rapture of soul, and to accompany sun, moon, and all heaven and the universe in their revolutions. Then, ah, then peering downwards from the ethereal heights and directing the eye of my intelligence as from a watchtower, I regarded the untold spectacle of all earthly things, and reckoned myself happy at having forcibly escaped the calamities of mortal life.

And yet there lurked near me that most grievous of evils, Envy [phthonos], with its hatred of all that is fair, which suddenly fell upon me, and did not cease dragging upon me until it had hurled me down into the vast sea of political cares, where I am still tossed about and unable even so much as to rise to the surface. But though I groan at my fate, I still struggle on, for implanted in my soul from early youth, I have a desire for education which ever has pity and compassion upon me, and lifts me up and elevates me. This it is by which I can sometimes raise my

---

[125] *An Introduction to Philo Judaeus*, pp. 52, 10f.

head, and by which, though the penetration of the eyes of my soul is dimmed by the mists of alien concerns, I can yet cast about with them in some measure upon my surroundings, while I long to suck the breast of life pure and unmixed with evils. And if unexpectedly there is temporary quiet and calm in the political tumults, I become winged and skim the waves, barely flying, and am blown along by the breezes of understanding, which often persuades me to run away as it were for a holiday from my pitiless masters, who are not only men but the great variety of practical affairs deluged upon me from all sides like a torrent. Still, even in such a condition, I ought to thank God that while I am inundated I am not sucked down into the depths. Rather, though in despair of my good hope I had considered the eyes of my soul to be incapacitated, now I open them and am flooded with the light of wisdom, so that I am not abandoned for the whole of my life to darkness. And so, behold, I dare not only read the sacred expositions of Moses, but even, with a passion for understanding, I venture to examine each detail, and to disclose and publish what is not known to the multitude.[126]

Coming from an ancient, this is a very impressive passage. It is a significant psychological confession that represents a capacity for honest self-reflection. He confesses that although he would much have preferred the state of permanent Olympian *sublimatio,* he was consumed by *phthonos,* envy, that forced him back to earth, into *coagulatio.* He does not tell us exactly how that envy functioned, but one can make a guess. Generally speaking, there are three basic targets of envy: fame, power, and pleasure. He tells us that he found himself envying others, presumably his own family, because his family included some people extremely prominent in worldly affairs. He found himself envying their practical functioning and the fruits of it, and this forced him back to earth. That indicates that his own unconscious forced upon him a degree of *coagulatio* that compensated for his natural tendency to an excessive one-sided *sublimatio,* and that is what gives him a modern flavor.

What is *coagulatio* in such circumstances? Matter and flesh, which are related to *coagulatio* symbolism, are also associated with evil. That means that in order to coagulate, one must embrace the shadow, which is always tinged with darkness to some extent. A classic example of this is found in Jung's letter to Richard Wilhelm, who was also a victim of one-sided *sublimatio:* one-sided, abstract, intellectual functioning. Wilhelm was ill, as if he were threatening to sublimate himself right out of existence, and Jung wrote him:

You are *too important* to our Western world. I must keep on telling you this. You mustn't melt away or otherwise disappear, or get ill, but wicked desires should pin

---

[126] *On the Special Laws,* III, 1-6, quoted in ibid., pp. 5f.

you to the earth so your work can go on.[127]

That is what happened to Philo: wicked desires coming up from his unconscious in the form of envy pinned him to the earth and probably gave him a longer life than he would otherwise have had. People who are too good often do not have a very long life.

For someone seeking perfection, envy is one of the seven deadly sins and is to be rigorously avoided, but for someone seeking completion, which is the goal of individuation, envy is evidence that something is lacking. If one envies something, or to put it more precisely, if the unconscious throws up feelings of envy (the ego does not manufacture them; it discovers them), it is an expression of a hunger for something that is lacking, that is needed. One may well discover later that one doesn't really want what one was envious about. In other words, what one is envious about may be carrying a projection or it may be symbolizing what the real lack is. Nonetheless, envy is a healthy hunger for what one needs, as long as one is conscious about it. If it is unconscious and hidden, then it can generate cunning and malice, and then it becomes truly evil. When it is conscious, it keeps us modest.

Philo's method of reconciling Hebrew scripture with Greek philosophy is called *allegoria*. The modern word is allegory. In modern usage, an allegory is a story which is interpreted as a kind of cryptogram in which each image stands for another entity on a different level of understanding. This was a well-known method among the Greeks, used to reconcile Homer and earlier mythological tales with later Greek rationalism. Philo did not create allegory, but he invented its use to connect Greek philosophy and Hebrew scripture.

The method was elaborated by two early writers named Heraclitus of Pontius (not the Heraclitus of chapter four), and Cornutus. Edwin Hatch writes:

> Both were Stoics, both are most probably assigned to the early part of the first century of our era. . . . Heraclitus [of Pontius] begins by the definite avowal of his apologetic purpose. His work is a vindication of Homer from the charge of impiety. "He would unquestionably be impious if he were not allegorical;" but as it is, "there is no stain of unholy fables in his words: they are pure and free from impiety." [Homer said some rather disagreeable things about the gods, but Heraclitus defends him, saying:] Apollo is the sun; the "far-darter" is the sun sending forth his rays: when it is said that Apollo slew men with his arrows, it is meant that there was a pestilence in the heat of summer-time. Athene is thought: when it is said that Athene came to Telamachus, it is meant only that the young man then first began

---

[127] *Letters,* vol. 1, p. 63.

to reflect upon the waste and profligacy of the suitors. . . . The story of Proteus and Eidothea is an allegory of the original formless matter taking many shapes: the story of Ares and Aphrodite and Hephaestus is a picture of iron subdued by fire, and restored to its original hardness by Poseidon, that is by water. [Of the other writer, Cornutus, Hatch says:] Cornutus writes in vindication not so much of the piety of the ancients as of their knowledge: they knew as much as men of later times, but they expressed it at greater length and by means of symbols. . . . The science of religion was to him, as it has been to some persons in modern days, an extension of the science of philology. The following are examples: Hermes (from *erein,* "to speak") is the power of speech which the gods sent from heaven as their peculiar and distinguishing gift to men. He is called the "conductor," because speech conducts one man's thought into his neighbor's soul. . . . He is the "leader of souls," because words soothe the soul to rest. . . . The serpents twined round his staff are a symbol of the savage natures that are calmed by words, and their discords gathered into harmony.[128]

The method of *allegoria,* then, was already employed around the time of Philo, but he makes very extensive use of it in relation to the Hebrew scriptures. Hatch comments:

But by far the most considerable monument of this mode of interpretation consists of the works of Philo. They are based throughout on the supposition of a hidden meaning. But they carry us into a new world. The hidden meaning is not physical, but metaphysical and spiritual. The seen is the veil of the unseen, a robe thrown over it which marks its contour, "and half conceals and half reveals the form within."[129]

For instance, in Philo's "On the Creation of the World," he applies allegory to the serpent in the Garden of Eden:

And these things are not mere fabulous inventions in which the race of poets and sophists delight, but are rather types shadowing forth some allegorical truth, according to some mystical explanation. And anyone who follows a reasonable train of conjecture will say with great propriety that the aforesaid serpent is a symbol of pleasure. . . . he is destitute of feet. . . . he uses lumps of clay for food. . . . he bears poison in his teeth. . . . the man devoted to pleasure is free from none of the afore-mentioned evils; for it is with difficulty that he can hardly raise his head, being weighed down and dragged down . . . [these people who are possessed by pleasure] . . . lick up the results of the labors of cooks and tavern-keepers. . . . [They are just like the serpent then in the way they lick the earth.][130]

---

[128] *The Influence of Greek Ideas and Usages Upon the Christian Church,* pp. 62f.

[129] Ibid., p. 67.

[130] Nahum N. Glatzer, ed., *The Essential Philo,* p. 36.

This method is of course not the same as the symbolic method of Jungian psychology, which distinguishes quite explicitly between a symbol of an unknown entity and a sign of known one. But the allegorical method in the hands of someone such as Philo can be ambiguous, so that at times it is not just a straightforward system of signs in which one image stands for something else. Used by Philo, it sometimes includes a bit of the symbolic as well. For example, when Philo discusses the marriage of Isaac to Rebecca, he says:

> Rebecca is Virtue or Sophia, interchangeably, and is clearly the "Female Principle." . . . She is so exalted a figure that her bracelets are sufficient to represent the entire cosmos which the immaterial Stream of God similarly wears. When she gives the servant to drink at the well it is the Logos itself which he receives.[131]

This is not strictly allegory, because Philo translates the figure of Sarah into such things as the female principle and the logos. Those are not completely known entities; they are symbols themselves, so that at least in part, some of Philo can be considered symbolic as that is understood psychologically.

Usually the allegory is stricter, as in Philo's interpretation of the brothers Isaac and Ishmael. Goodenough compares these two figures to two kinds of education. One kind is the standard, conventional, scientific education of the day, which is a preparation for higher, true education. The standard scientific education, he says, is the

> milk for spiritual babes . . . good, like childhood itself, only as a stage to pass through. When one remains [in that first level of education] . . . one remains in the material, since all [such study is] based upon sensory observations, and hence [is] earthly, not heavenly. With [this kind of study] . . . the soul cannot mate in the full sense. . . . Philo brings [to this] the allegory of Abraham, who first has relations with his concubine, Hagar, [representing] the introductory studies, and produces Ishmael, the sophist or pedagogue. These must be banished when the soul rises to appropriate the true knowledge and virtue, as Ishmael and Hagar had to be sent out from the presence of the fully developed Abraham and Sarah. Sarah, heavenly Sophia or Wisdom, has herself urged Hagar . . . [the introductory studies] upon Abraham in the early stages, but Abraham had later to divorce her to come into the higher life. Philo seems to me to be saying in his figurative way what we have been saying very much during the last years, that attention to, and development of, scientific knowledge is no guarantee, to say the least, of increase in our spiritual growth or perception.[132]

---

[131] Quoted in Goodenough, *An Introduction to Philo Judaeus*, pp. 143f.
[132] Ibid., pp. 135f.

Another, more symbolic example is Philo's interpretation of Abraham's migration. The eleventh chapter of Genesis tells us that Abraham migrated from his original home in Ur of the Chaldeans, and his first stop was at Haran, where the family settled for a time. Goodenough comments:

> Abraham migrated from Chaldea, Philo explains, when he rejected the philosophy which made the material world the ultimate form of existence. In the new land, Charan [Haran], he thus began to study the world afresh and quickly concluded that there must be a mind behind the material aspects of man. When he got this conception, God could then take the first step in revelation. This first revelation was the empowering of Abraham's mind to run up and apprehend a nature or existence quite beyond matter, to apprehend even the being who was beyond both material and immaterial natures and who had created both. As a result of this Abraham's name was changed to indicate he had become the Sage, the ideal man of antiquity. Abraham was now ready for the next step, which was union with Sophia or Virtue, presented quite as a mythological figure and represented in the story by Sarah.[133] [Then, as a demonstration of Abraham's new status, he moved again, to Palestine.]

As we read Philo, we find the same terms that have been discussed here in earlier chapters: *physis, nous, logos, psyche, pronoia.* Usually Philo used translations rather than these Greek terms, but he elaborates them quite fruitfully. Consider, for example, his meditation on the word *psyche:*

> We have ourselves, and all that goes to make these selves, as a loan. I, indeed, am a combination of soul and body *[psyche* and *soma],* seeming to have in mind *[nous]* reason (or speech) and sense perception, yet I find that none of these is my own property. For where was my body before I was born, and whither will it go when I have died? And what has become of the distinct life-periods of this "self," which appears to be a constant? Where is the babe that once I was, the little boy, the stripling, the young adolescent, the youth, the young buck, the young man, and the adult? Whence came the soul and whither will it go, and how long will it live with *us?* Can we tell what is its essential nature? And when did we come to possess it? Before birth? But then we did not exist. After death? But then we, who, in our junction with our bodies, are mixtures and have qualities, shall not exist, but shall push on into the rebirth, by which becoming joined to immaterial things, we shall become unmixed and without qualities.[134]

Philo uses the terms *physis* and *nous* in another passage:

> But Moses, who had early reached the very summits of philosophy, and who would learn from the oracles of God the most numerous and important of the prin-

---

[133] Ibid., p. 141.

[134] Ibid., pp. 114f.

ciples of nature *[physis]* was well aware that it is indispensable that in all existing things there must be an active cause and a passive subject [that is right out of Aristotle]; and that the active cause is the intellect *[nous]* of the universe, thoroughly unadulterated and thoroughly unmixed, superior to virtue and superior to science, superior even to abstract good or abstract beauty; while the passive subject is something inanimate and incapable of motion by any intrinsic power of its own, but having been set in motion and fashioned, and endowed with life by the intellect *[nous]*, became transformed into that most perfect work, this world. And those who describe it as being uncreated, do, without being aware of it, cut off the most useful and necessary of all the qualities which tend to produce piety, namely providence *[pronoia]*: for reason proves that the father and creator has a care for that which has been created; for a father is anxious for the life of his children, and a workman aims at the duration of his works, and employs every device imaginable to ward off everything that is pernicious or injurious, and is desirous by every means in his power to provide everything which is useful or profitable for them. But with regard to that which has not been created, there is no feeling of interest as if it were his own in the breast of him who has not created it.[135]

This is an interesting argument for the creation of the world. It was a common notion of the Greek philosophers that the universe was uncreated, but Philo insists that it must have been created, that it would be a pernicious doctrine to state that the world was uncreated, because that would mean that it had no creator who would be concerned to take care of his creation.

Philo makes the further argument that Plato's world of ideas (the *kosmos noetos*, translated the "intelligible world"), was the first thing God created on the first day. The sense world was brought into being afterward:

For God, as apprehending beforehand, as a God must do, for there could not exist a good imitation without a good model, and that of the things perceptible to the external senses nothing could be faultless which was not fashioned with reference to some archetypal idea [in Philo's text that is not the psychological term "archetype," but the word *paradigma*] conceived by the intellect, when he had determined to create this visible world, previously formed that one which is perceptible only by the intellect, in order that in so using an incorporeal model formed as far as possible in the image of God, he might then make this corporeal world, a younger likeness of the elder creation, which should embrace as many different genera perceptible to the external senses, as the other world contains of those which are visible only to the intellect.[136]

... And if any one were to desire to use more undisguised terms, he would not call the world, which is perceptible only to the intellect, anything else but the reason of God, already occupied in the creation of the world; [the word translated as

---

[135] Glatzer, *The Essential Philo*, pp. 2f.

[136] Ibid., p. 4.

"reason" is *logos]* for neither is a city, while only perceptible to the intellect, any-thing else but the reason of the architect, who is already designing to build one perceptible to the external senses, on the model of that which is so only to the in-tellect—this is the doctrine of Moses, not mine. Accordingly he, when recording the creation of man in words which follow, asserts expressly that he was made in the image of God—and if the image be a part of the image, then manifestly so is the entire form, namely, the whole of this world perceptible by the external senses, which is a greater imitation of the divine image than the human form is.[137]

Philo says here essentially the same thing as Jung, who wrote that "matter rep-resents the *concreteness* of God's thoughts."[138]

Philo also takes up the theme of God's creation of the world:

Guided by his own sole will, [he] decided that it was fitting to benefit with unlim-ited and abundant favors a nature *[physis]* which, without the divine gift, was un-able of itself to partake of any good thing; but he benefits it, not according to the greatness of his own graces, for they are illimitable and eternal, but according to the power of that which is benefited to receive his graces. For the capacity of that which is created to receive benefits does not correspond to the natural power of God to confer them; since his powers are infinitely greater, and the thing created being not sufficiently powerful to receive all their greatness would have sunk un-der it, if he had not measured his bounty, allotting to each in due proportion that which was poured upon it.[139]

This idea is interesting in its psychological applications. Translated into psy-chological terminology, it says that the collective unconscious carefully meas-ures the magnitude of its flow into the ego in order not to swamp it with an input beyond its powers of assimilation. In general that is true; the healthy psyche does indeed function such that the unconscious does not inundate the ego; there are checks on it. There are certain individuals, however, for whom such protec-tive instincts do not seem to operate. They are subject to inundation by the un-conscious; more flows in than they can possibly assimilate. Those are the occa-sions of psychosis. The assumption is that the built-in protective mechanisms are defective in those individuals, which is probably the basis of the genetic factor in schizophrenia.

There is a widespread perception, with some truth to it, that genius and mad-ness are very close together, and that sometimes one merges into the other. This

---

[137] Ibid., p. 6.

[138] "A Psychological Approach to the Dogma of the Trinity," *Psychology and Religion,* CW 11, par. 252.

[139] Glatzer, *The Essential Philo,* p. 6.

would seem to be an occasion where the protective mechanisms are weak and, in some circumstances, the inundation from the unconscious can have a very creative effect, as the inundation of the Nile fertilizes Egypt. The difference between a rich, fertilizing flood and a disastrous one may not be very great, which would account for certain highly creative people who seem right on the verge of psychosis and sometimes go over the edge. Hölderlin is a good example of that.

Philo also has an interesting observation concerning the quaternity:

> There is also another power of the number four which is a most wonderful one to speak of and to contemplate. For it was this number that first displayed the nature of the solid cube, the numbers before four being assigned only to incorporeal things. For it is according to the unit [one] that the thing is reckoned which is spoken of in geometry as a point: and a line is spoken of according to the number two, because it is arranged by nature from a point; and a line is length without breadth. But when breadth is added to it, it becomes a superficies [a plane] which is arranged according to the number three. And a superficies, when compared with the nature of a solid cube, wants one thing, namely depth, and when this one thing is added to the three, it becomes four. On which account it has happened that this number is a thing of great importance inasmuch as from an incorporeal substance perceptible only by intellect, it has led us on to a comprehension of a body divisible in a threefold manner, . . . first perceived by the external senses.[140]

That is Jungian psychology. In order to understand its background, one must be familiar with the ideas in a work of Plato which Jung calls "the mystery-laden *Timaeus* of Plato." It is a late dialogue in which Plato describes in more or less symbolic terms how the demiurge created the universe. Jung discusses this work in his essay on the Trinity. He begins by quoting Plato *(Timaeus,* section 31B):

> Hence the god, when he began to put together the body of the universe, set about making it of fire and earth. But two things alone cannot be satisfactorily united without a third; for there must be some bond between them drawing them together. And of all bonds the best is that which makes itself and the terms it connects a unity in the fullest sense; and it is of the nature of a continued geometrical proportion to effect this most perfectly. For whenever, of three numbers, the middle one between any two that are either solids or planes [i.e., cubes or squares] is such that, as the first is to it, so is it to the last, and conversely as the last is to the middle, so is the middle to the first, then since the middle becomes first and last, and again the last and first become middle, in that way all will necessarily come to play the same part towards one another, and by so doing they will all make a unity. . . . [141]

---

[140] Ibid., p. 13.

[141] "A Psychological Approach to the Dogma of the Trinity," *Psychology and Religion,* CW 11, par. 181.

Jung comments:

> Accordingly, the two-dimensional connection is not yet a physical reality, for a plane without extension in the third dimension is only an *abstract thought*. [That is exactly what Philo said.] If it is to become a physical reality, three dimensions, and therefore two means, are required. . . .
>
> It is interesting to note that Plato begins by representing the union of opposites two-dimensionally, as an intellectual problem to be solved by thinking, but then comes to see that its solution does not add up to reality. In the former case we have to do with a self-subsistent triad, and in the latter with a quaternity. This was the dilemma that perplexed the alchemists for more than a thousand years, and, as the "axiom of Maria Prophetissa" (the Jewess or Copt), it appears in modern dreams, and is also found in psychology as the opposition between the functions of consciousness, three of which are fairly well differentiated, while the fourth, undifferentiated, "inferior" function is undomesticated, unadapted, uncontrolled, and primitive. Because of its contamination with the collective unconscious, it possesses archaic and mystical qualities, and is the complete opposite of the most differentiated function. . . . Hence the opening words of the *Timaeus*—"One, two, three—but where, my dear Timaeus, is the fourth . . . ?"—fall familiarly upon the ears of the psychologist.[142]

This is the same issue that Philo presents. It refers to the psychological fact that one does not experience the psyche as an empirical reality, as opposed to an abstract thought, until the fourth function comes into consciousness. Knowing the psyche as an empirical reality requires the living, conscious encounter with all four functions. That is the basic theme of the Axiom of Maria, mentioned earlier, which is formulated as "one becomes two, two becomes three, and out of the third comes the one, as the fourth." This means that when the fourth, inferior function arrives on the scene, it brings with it the totality of the Self. That is what is meant by "the one as the fourth." This theme is referred to again and again in dream images in all kinds of settings with all kinds of objects, where there are three things of a similar nature, plus a fourth thing that is offbeat somehow, of a different nature from the other three. One encounters such images all the time, even in people who are quite far from full individuation, even in children.

The fact that psychic reality comes into living experience only with the emergence of the fourth function corresponds to Philo's personal experience of *coagulatio,* in which envy brought him back down to earth. *Coagulatio* takes place by embracing the shadow. The fourth function is the inferior, undevel-

---

[142] Ibid., pars. 181f.

oped, despised part of the personality that is always tinged with evil. That is not a euphemism, because it is real evil, not just harmless darkness. That is why those who seek individuation, who really, earnestly have as their goal completeness rather than perfection, are particularly subject to shadow projections. That is what has happened to Jung. It is the inevitable accompaniment of seeking completion rather than perfection. The shadow projectors always have perfection as their goal, not necessarily acknowledged as such, but that is what it reveals itself to be.

It is symbolically significant that Philo is the first ancient author to use the word "archetype":

> So then after all the other things, as has been said before, Moses says that man was made in the image and likeness of God. And he says well; for nothing that is born on earth is more resembling God than man. And let no one think that he is able to judge of this likeness from the characters of the body: for neither is God a being with the form of a man nor is the human body like the form of God; but the resemblance is spoken of with reference to the most important part of the soul, namely the mind [the *nous*]: for the mind which exists in each individual has been created after the likeness of that one mind [the one *nous*] which is in the universe as its primitive model [as its *archetypos*].[143]

Jung refers to this in a letter written in 1948 to Victor White, saying:

> By the way: the earliest use of the word [*archetypos*] I have just found occurs in Philo: *De Opificio mundi* [Of the Creation of the World], 1, par. 69, referring to the [images of God, in respect of the mind, the sovereign element of the soul]. Hitherto I had believed that it first occurs in the *Corpus Hermeticum* . . . . [St. Augustine] does not use "archetypus" as I once erroneously surmised, only the idea, but it occurs in *Dionysius Areopagita.*[144]

This connection between Jung and Philo is especially important symbolically, as it underscores the significance of the fact that Philo's method was a kind of a foreshadowing of Jung's.

---

[143] In Glatzer, *The Essential Philo*, p. 19.

[144] *Letters,* vol. 1, p. 507.

11
Plotinus

Plotinus lived from 204 to 270 A.D., 200 years after Philo and almost 600 years after Plato, whom Plotinus considered to be his master. Plotinus is the father of neo-Platonism, a major school of late Greek philosophy. Although he modestly stated that he was just extracting what was already in Plato, it is generally considered that he made major contributions and additions to Plato's doctrine. He systematized and pragmatized it, and he brought it into relationship to human experience in a way that Plato had not done.

His body of work exists because his student Porphyry edited all of his writings, leaving them in a form that could be transmitted. Porphyry also prefaced the works, the six *Enneads,* with a biography of Plotinus. According to Porphyry, Plotinus was born and reared in Alexandria. At the age of twenty-seven, he fell in love with philosophy in a sudden awakening to his calling. He gave himself over for eleven years to the Alexandrian teacher Ammonius Saccus—an apprenticeship in philosophy—and then he proceeded on his own. At forty, he moved from Alexandria to Rome, where he spent the rest of his life. Porphyry says:

> Not a few men and women of position [in Rome], on the approach of death, had left their boys and girls, with all their property, in his care, feeling that with Plotinus for guardian the children would be in holy hands. His house therefore was filled with lads and lasses. . . .
>
> He always found time for those that came to submit returns of the children's property, and he looked closely to the accuracy of the accounts. "Until the young people take to philosophy," he would say, "their fortunes and revenues must be kept intact for them."[145]

That is a particularly enlightening glimpse into the personal life of Plotinus. In reading his philosophy, one has the impression that he is so other-worldly that he would not pay much attention to material issues, but it is clear that he was a man of great kindliness and that in his practical life he gave due respect to the reality of matter. Porphyry says that he had no enemies whatsoever.

On one occasion, an Egyptian priest evoked Plotinus' "presiding spirit." A divinity appeared, and the priest said, "You are singularly graced; the guiding

---

[145] Steven MacKenna, trans., *Plotinus: The Enneads*, p. 7.

spirit within you is not of the lower degree, but a God,"[146] indicating his magnanimity in the original meaning of that word, his *megalothymia,* his greatness of soul.

Plotinus' basic system is a magnificent philosophical fantasy of the structure of the universe. He was clearly an individual of extraordinary imagination and intuition. It is as though his intuitive gifts perceived the basic structure of the psyche, which he then read into the universe. Since, as Jung puts it, there was no epistemological criticism in those days, this unfolding fantasy can provide us with basic data in which the psyche is describing its own structure and nature, thus making the material relevant today.

He conceived of the universe as a fourfold structure, although he paid so little attention to matter that it was really a threefold structure, with peripheral remarks about matter. At the very beginning is *hen* or what is called the One, the origin from which everything else emanates or radiates or descends. Next comes *nous,* the divine mind, or what was called from earlier terminology, the *kosmos noetos,* the intelligible world. Below that emanates the psyche, the soul, which is thought of in two portions: an upper aspect of the soul, oriented to that which is above it, to *nous,* and the lower aspect, which penetrates nature and matter. Then, finally, at the bottom of the structure, although Plotinus gives it very little attention, is *hyle,* or matter, which corresponds to the *kosmos aisthetos* of earlier terminology, meaning the sensible world.

This is very similar, in broad outlines, to the structure of the psyche as Jung has represented it, keeping in mind that in analysis the psyche is discovered by going upwards from below, rather than downwards from above, as Plotinus has it. In analysis one starts with the ego, equivalent to the level of matter, and works toward the Self. The process goes first through the shadow, the ego's double, and then into the first truly autonomous entity, the soul figure, the anima or animus, which provides a connecting link to the archetypal psyche or the collective unconscious. The collective unconscious in turn has as its center and totality, the Self.

As Jung says, emphasizing the importance of the ego:

Matter represents the *concreteness* of God's thoughts and is, therefore, the very thing that makes individuation possible, with all its consequences.[147]

---

[146] Ibid., p. 8.

[147] "A Psychological Approach to the Dogma of the Trinity," *Psychology and Religion,* CW 11, par. 252.

Matter is symbolically equivalent to ego, and the emphasis on it is the great distinction between Jungian psychology and the later Greek philosophers, who are inclined to a one-sided spiritual *sublimatio.*

The classical scholar A.H. Armstrong has some particularly valuable things to say about Plotinus:

> The philosophy of Plotinus is an account of an ordered structure of living reality, which proceeds eternally from its transcendent First Principle, the One or Good, and descends in an unbroken succession of stages from the Divine Intellect and the Forms therein through Soul with its various levels of experience and activity to the last and lowest realities, the forms of bodies: and it is also a showing of the way by which the soul of man . . . can experience and be active on every level of being, is able, if it will, to ascend by a progressive purification and simplification to that union with the Good which alone can satisfy it. There are two movements in Plotinus's universe, one of outgoing from unity to an ever-increasing multiplicity and the other of return to unity and unification.[148]

Armstrong continues by discussing the One. (Here we must keep in mind that this will be a naive description of the nature of the Self, before the Self had been discovered.) The One is also called the Good, indicating the *sublimatio* tendency, because in this terminology, as "the Good," it is stripped of its opposite, although in all other respects it has the opposite:

> Plotinus insists that the . . . good is beyond being, for being is always `being something,' some one particular defined and limited thing . . . and the One is not a thing, nor yet the sum of particular realities. . . . [It is absolute being, containing all definite realities in their archetypal form, but prior to their realization, because their realization occurs in *nous.]* Again, Plotinus insists that the One does not think, because thought for him always implies a certain duality, a distinction of thought and object of thought, and it is this that he is concerned to exclude in speaking of the One. . . . [So thinking only takes place in the *nous,* but in the One it does not take place.][149]

This is very similar to Jung's description of the paradoxical God-image as an expression of the Self, prior to consciousness. Consciousness splits subject and object. There can be no actual thought process until there is a thinker and a thing thought. Conscious discrimination has to take place, and it takes place at the level of matter, of the ego. This makes matter crucial, since it concretizes and brings into visible reality God's latent thoughts.

---

[148] Armstrong, trans. and ed., *Plotinus,* pp. 27f.

[149] Ibid., pp. 31f.

Armstrong continues, concerning the *nous* or the intelligible world:

> From the One proceeds the first great derived reality, Nous, the Divine Mind which is also the World of Forms or Ideas, so the totality of true being in the Platonic sense. . . . The way in which Nous proceeds from the One . . . is rather loosely and inadequately described as emanation.[150]

Plotinus often uses the metaphor of the sun emanating light. It is thought of as a radiating phenomenon, and corresponds to what in Jungian terms is the collective unconscious or the archetypal psyche, whose contents are the archetypes. They are the visible and particularized manifestations of the Self, which in its pure form has a kind of generalized numinosity. That numinosity is transmitted into the archetypes, so that in encountering an archetype one experiences the numinosity of the Self radiating through it. This unity of thought and form in a single reality which Armstrong describes is the nature of the *nous*.

Armstrong comments that the middle Platonists "had already taught that the Forms [the Platonic forms] were the 'thoughts of God,' "[151] so that idea, which appears in Thomas Aquinas, was already operative with Plotinus:

> But Plotinus goes a good deal beyond this . . . [because the *nous* or the divine mind] is no longer a structure, logically or mathematically conceived, of static universal norms, but an organic living community of interpenetrating beings which are at once Forms and intelligences, all "awake and alive," in which every part thinks and therefore in a real sense *is* the whole.[152]

This is an accurate description of the archetypal psyche one encounters in Jungian analysis. The Platonic image was a static one. Plato did not think of the forms, the *eide,* as organic entities with their own purpose, their own energy and direction. He thought of them as static abstractions; it was more an intellectual perception, whereas Plotinus is elaborating his notion from living experience. He had a very rich inner life, of which one may find hints in his writings. It is apropos that he is called the "father of mystics."

Armstrong says about the term *psyche* or soul:

> Soul . . . is the great intermediary between the worlds of intellect and sense [i.e., matter]. . . . It proceeds from Nous and returns upon it. . . . Plotinus hesitates a good deal over the question of whether . . . [the soul's] going out from [the world of *nous* in order to give] form and order [to] the material universe is a fall, an act

---

[150] Ibid., p. 33.

[151] Ibid., p. 35.

[152] Ibid.

of illegitimate self-will and self-assertion, or a good and necessary part of the universal order. [Concerning this lower universe,] Plotinus is reluctant to admit it, [but he actually has] a fourth distinct hypostasis, and [it] has its special name, Nature.[153]

This "nature" corresponds to *hyle,* matter. It appears that Plotinus, without quite realizing it, is presenting us with a quaternity, although he talks only about a trinity, and his trinitarian thinking was so definite that many of the Christian theologians took it over and assimilated it into the Christian Trinity.

Plotinus discusses the question of how, in a "downward process," an individual soul gets alienated from its origin:

> [There comes a time when the soul comes to the level] of individuality . . . [and such souls then] wish to be independent. They are tired, you might say, of living with someone else. Each steps down into its own individuality.
>
> When a soul remains for long in this withdrawal and estrangement from the whole, with never a glance towards the intelligible [when it has lost its connection to the One], it becomes a thing fragmented, isolated, and weak. Activity lacks concentration. Attention is tied to particulars. Severed from the whole, the soul clings to the part; to this one sole thing buffeted about by a whole worldful of things, has it turned and given itself. Adrift now from the whole, it manages even this particular thing with difficulty, its care of it compelling attention to externals, presence to the body, the deep penetration of the body. Thus comes about what is called "loss of wings" or the "chaining of the soul."[154]

This chaining of the soul is a basic theme encountered commonly in dream work and in mythology, such as the image of a beautiful damsel chained to a rock. It is an image of the soul that has fallen into matter or egohood and has lost, as Plotinus describes it, its connection to its origin in the One. He goes on:

> Its [ways] no longer are the ways of innocence in which, with The [upper] Soul, it presided over the higher realms. Life above was better by far than this. A thing fallen, chained, at first barred off from intelligence and living only by sensation, the soul is, as they say, in tomb or cavern pent.
>
> Yet its higher part remains. Let the soul, taking its lead from memory, *[anamnesis,* recollection], merely "think on essential being" and its shackles are loosed and it soars.[155]

One of the nice things about Plotinus is that he writes almost like a novelist;

---

[153] Ibid., p. 37.

[154] Elmer O'Brien, *The Essential Plotinus,* p. 66.

[155] Ibid.

he is so wonderfully articulate that his writing is very close to the modern. For example:

> How is it, then, that souls forget the divinity that begot them so that—divine by nature, divine by origin—they now know neither divinity nor self?
>
> This evil that has befallen them has its source in self-will, in being born, in becoming different, in desiring to be independent. . . . And when they have gone a great distance, they even forget that they came from [divinity]. Like children separated from their family since birth and educated away from home, they are ignorant now of their parentage and therefore of their identity.[156]

Plotinus goes on to discuss the state of alienation, which was also a theme in the teachings of the Gnostics. These alienated souls forget their worth:

> Ignorance of origin is caused by excessive valuation of sense objects and disdain of self, for to pursue something and hold it dear implies acknowledgment of inferiority to what is pursued. As soon as a soul thinks it is worth less than things subject to birth and death, considers itself least honorable and enduring of all, it can no longer grasp the nature and power of the divinity. A soul in such condition can be turned about and led back to the world above and the supreme existent . . . by a twofold discipline: by showing it the low value of the things it esteems at present, and by informing—reminding!—it [recollection] of its nature and worth.[157]

One can recognize this twofold discipline in psychological terms: showing the soul the low value of the things it esteems at present corresponds to analyzing projections, and reminding the soul of its nature and worth corresponds to analytic anamnesis, which involves a study of the products of the unconscious, thus gradually opening up and reconnecting the ego to its origin. These are two quite explicit parallels between Plotinian philosophy and Jungian psychology.

Plotinus' essay "On Beauty" is perhaps his best known. It is an elaboration of a passage in Plato's *Symposium.* In this passage, Socrates speaks about the nature of love and in the course of his presentation, he describes what Diotima, an old wise woman, taught him. This is equivalent to a dream within a dream: Plato uses Socrates as his mouthpiece and, in the dialogue, Socrates uses Diotima as his mouthpiece, indicating the particular depth from which this wisdom comes. At the end of this famous passage, Diotima is telling Socrates the procedure by which love for beautiful objects and people is gradually transformed into love of the divine—how to make the transfer of libido from love of the sensory world to love of God. She summarizes it as follows:

---

[156] Ibid., p. 91.
[157] Ibid., pp. 91f.

"Begin from the beauties of earth and mount upwards for the sake of that other beauty, using these as steps only, and from one going on to two, and from two to all fair forms, and from fair forms to fair practices, and from fair practices to fair notions, until from fair notions he arrives at the notion of absolute beauty, and at last knows what the essence of beauty is. This, my dear Socrates," said the stranger of Mantineia [i.e., Diotima], "is that life above all others which man should live, in the contemplation of beauty absolute; a beauty which if you once beheld, you would see not to be after the measure of gold, and garments, and fair boys and youths, whose presence now entrances you; and you and many a one would be content to live seeing them only and conversing with them without meat or drink, if that were possible—you only want to look at them [the divine beauties] and to be with them. But what if man had eyes to see the true beauty—the divine beauty, I mean, pure and clear and unalloyed, not clogged with the pollutions of mortality and all the colors and vanities of human life—thither looking, and holding converse with the true beauty, simple and divine?[158]

This is a formula for *sublimatio,* and it can be applied to all the archetypes, not just the archetype of beauty. It is similar to the analytic procedure of perceiving the archetypal patterns that lie behind the particular experiences and particular symptoms and preoccupations of the patient and of the imagery in the dream. When dreams start speaking in archetypal images, one looks for the general form, the archetype, behind the particular. The unconscious then wants to be understood in those terms. One pursues it because the goal is a broader context and perspective, recognition of the general collective surrounding one's personal experience. Finding this *sublimatio* aspect is releasing, but of course the personal must not be neglected. The personal is amplified by the archetypal. By following *sublimatio* in its strict form, the way Plato and Plotinus did, the goal will be perfection and not wholeness. For Jungian analysis, *sublimatio* is one aspect of individuation, but not its goal, because it does not unite the opposites. *Sublimatio* must be followed by *coagulatio.*

It is evident, however, that the idealization of *sublimatio,* which started with Plato and is so prominent in Plotinus, is really the central theme of the Christian aeon. It is the basic image underlying Platonism, Stoicism and Christianity. As Jung points out, the Christian and Gnostic redeemers start out in heaven, descend to earth and teach humanity how to ascend to heaven, to which they then return. By contrast, the alchemical redeemer, the Philosophers' Stone, has a different itinerary. According to the Emerald Tablet of Hermes, "He ascends from earth to heaven and descends again to earth, and receives the power of Above

---

[158] Quoted in ibid., pp. 190f.

and Below."[159] This is a totally different movement. The first process is an essentially *sublimatio* movement, the other is an essentially *coagulatio* one.

Related to the symbolism of *sublimatio* versus *coagulatio* is the question of matter as evil, a theme that runs through all the ancient material. In psychological terms, the question becomes: is ego development rooted in evil? Is incarnated human existence the action of a good creator-God, or is it the result of a "fall" or a "crime" due to rebellious human self-will?

To return for a moment to the discussion above in chapter two: according to Anaximander, all discriminated particular things have to pay reparation for the injustice of their coming into existence. Similarly, Empedocles' view, which was part of the Orphic viewpoint, was that incarnated souls had to undergo purification to be redeemed from primal crimes. There was also the later Gnostic idea that flesh and matter are prisons imposed by an evil demiurge.

In the passage cited earlier, Plotinus was not quite clear on that question; he fluctuated. Armstrong says in regard to Plotinus' attitude:

> His attitude to the visible universe was utterly opposed to that of the Gnostics. For them it was an evil prison, vitiated in its very nature, produced as a result of the fall of a spiritual power, with which man (or at least the Gnostic) who had come into it from a higher world as a result of that fall had absolutely nothing in common, which he utterly rejected and sought to escape from by means of the *gnosis*. For Plotinus, in this entirely true to Plato's doctrine, the visible universe was good, an essential part of the nature of things, not the result of any fall or error but of the spontaneous expansion of the divine goodness to fill all possible being, made by divine intelligence as the best possible material image of the spiritual universe. Man was akin to and should venerate as nobler than himself the divine souls which moved the stars. . . . He certainly belonged by right to the spiritual world and should seek to return there and transcend the material even while in the body: but he should do it without resentment or impatience or denial of the goodness of the visible world and his own real duties there.[160]

On the other hand, Plotinus' doctrine of matter as darkness and the principle of evil is in language and thought much like Gnosticism, indicating that Plotinus did not really solve his ambivalence, which is in his favor psychologically.

Matter and body are symbolically equal to ego, so that depreciation of matter is equivalent to criminalizing the ego. A corollary issue is the question of what is the ego's responsibility for itself. Plotinus speaks to this. Paul Henry, a Jesuit writing as a Catholic thinker, comments:

---

[159] Quoted in "The Spirit Mercurius," *Alchemical Studies,* CW 13, par. 280.

[160] Armstrong, *Plotinus,* pp. 24f.

Neither Socrates nor Plato took sufficient note of the will-factor. In their teaching there is no place—as moreover there is none in Aristotle—for sin and plenary responsibility. In this matter Plotinus strove—unsuccessfully, as he realized—to bring harmony into contradictory affirmations of Plato: on the one hand, the soul is free, self-impelled, responsible in its "fall" . . . on the other hand, its descent is necessary for insuring the government, life, and ordering of the universe. . . .

The central doctrine of Socrates is that virtue is knowledge. Plotinus agrees. The Intellect, with which the soul in the higher phase of its life is identified, is without sin and strictly incapable of sinning. "Vice is not a perversion of intelligence, but a condition in which this activity is absent or dormant. . . . [So that, for Plato and Socrates, there is no such thing as sin. There is only ignorance, not knowing any better.] Wrongdoing is not so much rebellion and defiance as bewilderment and weariness." Where wrongdoing simply does not exist, there can of course be no place either for pardon and expiation or for salvation. [Instead of penance and repentance, it is just a matter of forgetfulness. One forgot what one originally knew.] . . . The contrast with the Biblical revelation and with certain lines of thought in the Ancient Near East is complete. Where the Christian sees tragic contradiction, the Neoplatonist diagnoses a weakness or incapacity.[161]

The question of the ego's sinfulness and responsibility for itself is an important issue in psychotherapy. There are, of course, different attitudes about this matter and one does not hear too much talk about sin and responsibility in most schools of psychotherapy. The issue can be understood as deriving from the differing levels of ego development. A patient's stage of ego development determines what aspect the analyst should emphasize.

In general, the young ego requires the discipline of taking responsibility for its own impulses. If one feels no guilt for indulging antisocial impulses, one is on the way to a character disorder. Guilt feelings are appropriate when one is dealing with infantile attitudes and with character disorders. In such cases, the analyst is obliged to provide moral education in order for the ego to develop personal responsibility. Behavior such as shoplifting and tax evasion, without accompanying guilt, must be confronted with a moral attitude and labeled as criminal. The moral rule should be what Kant established in his categorical imperative: behavior which cannot be used as a universal rule of behavior for all without damage to society, is immoral and is not admissible. If the ego lapses into such actions, it needs to feel guilty, a process that separates the ego from the shadow, and a task which involves a certain amount of repression and splitting.

At a later stage, when the shadow is to be assimilated, there is a shift in approach. Not that criminal behavior is condoned, but rather the individual comes

---

[161] In MacKenna, *Plotinus: The Enneads.* p. xxxviii.

to recognize that criminal and shadow tendencies are a part of one's basic nature. Nobody can make self-righteous claims to moral superiority. Shadow assimilation takes place in this way. It keeps one modest and connected to fellow human beings, releasing one from shadow projection. In this late stage Jung's statement applies: "Man's suffering does not derive from his sins but from the maker of his imperfections, the paradoxical God."[162]

Jung makes an important reference to Plotinus in *Mysterium Coniunctionis*, discussing the alchemist Gerhard Dorn's text on the *coniunctio:*

> Whether Dorn also knew Plotinus is questionable. In his fourth Ennead Plotinus discusses the problem of whether all individuals are merely one soul, and he believes he has good grounds for affirming this question. I mention Plotinus because he is an earlier witness to the idea of the *unus mundus.* The "unity of the soul" rests empirically on the basic psychic structure common to all souls, which, though not visible and tangible like the anatomical structure, is just as evident as it.[163]

What Jung does here is to bring Plotinus in as evidence for the reality of the collective unconscious. The "Ninth Tractate" of the fourth *Ennead* contains a precursor to the concept of the collective unconscious. Jung refers to this doctrine of Plotinus as a parallel to his notion of synchronicity. Plotinus writes:

> That the Soul of every individual is one thing we deduce from the fact that it is present entire at every point of the body—the sign of veritable unity—not some part of it here and another part there. In all sensitive beings the sensitive soul is an omnipresent unity. . . .
>
> Now are we to hold similarly that your soul and mine and all are one, and that the same thing is true of the universe, the soul in all the several forms of life being one soul, not parcelled out in separate items, but an omnipresent identity?
>
> If the soul in me is a unity, why need that in the universe be otherwise, seeing that there is no longer any question of bulk or body? And if that, too, is one soul, and yours and mine belong to it, then yours and mine must also be one: and if, again, the soul of the universe and mine depend from one soul, once more all must be one. . . . Reflection tells us that we are in sympathetic relation to each other, suffering, overcome, at the sight of pain, naturally drawn to forming attachments; and all this can be due only to some unity among us.
>
> Again, if spells and other forms of magic are efficient even at a distance to attract us into sympathetic relations, the agency can be no other than the one soul.
>
> A quiet word induces changes in a remote object, and makes itself heard at vast distances—proof of the oneness of all things within the one soul.[164]

---

[162] "Jung and Religious Belief," *The Symbolic Life,* CW 18, par. 1681.

[163] CW 14, par. 761.

[164] In MacKenna, *Plotinus: The Enneads,* pp. 364ff.

Today, we take the same phenomena and call them by another name: synchronicity.[165] It is interesting that Plotinus was not above drawing in magical spells as evidence for his philosophical ideas.

Plotinus, from his later historical viewpoint, further clarified the Stoic notion of *autarchia,* self-sufficiency or self-rule, which was an important concept for the Stoics, and was supposed to be one of the qualities of the Stoic sage. The Stoics had not made a distinction between the ego and the Self, so that they were implying that the self-sufficiency of the ego was a virtue—something which would now be seen as an inflated condition. For Plotinus *autarchia* is clearly a quality not of the ego, but of the One:

> There must be something that is fully self-sufficient *[autarchia].* That is The One; it alone, within and without, is without need. It needs nothing outside itself either to exist, to achieve well-being, or to be sustained in existence. As it is the cause of the other things, how could it owe its existence to them? And how could it derive its well-being from outside itself since its well-being is not something contingent but is its very nature? And, since it does not occupy space, how can it need support or foundation? What needs foundation is the material mass which, unfounded, falls. [Here one can read "ego," What needs foundation is the ego, which, without foundation, falls.] The One is the foundation of all other things and gives them, at one and the same time, existence and location; what needs locating is not self-sufficing.[166]

Plotinus also elaborates on the Platonic term *eidos*—idea or form. He affirms the position that *eide* exist for individuals. Plato defined the *eide* as the general defining forms for particular species, but Plotinus takes it a step further and says that there is an eternal form, an eternal *eidos,* for each individual. This corresponds to the Christian notion of an immortal soul, to the idea of having one's name written in heaven, and it parallels our psychological understanding of the nature of the Self, as contrasted to the ego. In the final sentence of "Answer to Job," Jung expresses this:

> Even the enlightened person remains what he is, and is never more than his own limited ego before the One who dwells within him, whose form has no knowable boundaries, who encompasses him on all sides, fathomless as the abysms of the earth and vast as the sky.[167]

---

[165] See "Synchronicity: An Acausal Connecting Principle," *The Structure and Dynamics of the Psyche,* CW 8.

[166] In O'Brien, ed., *The Essential Plotinus,* p. 81.

[167] *Psychology and Religion,* CW 11, par. 758.

Similarly, Plotinus in his final *Ennead* sums up the relation of the ego to the One:

The One does not aspire to us, to move around us; we aspire to it, to move around it. Actually, we always move around it; but we do not always look. We are like a chorus grouped about a conductor who allow their attention to be distracted by the audience. If, however, they were to turn towards their conductor, they would sing as they should and would really be with him. We are always around The One. If we were not, we would dissolve and cease to exist. Yet our gaze does not remain fixed upon *the* One. When we look at it, we then attain the end of our desires and find rest. Then it is that, all discord past, we dance an inspired dance around it.[168]

---

[168] O'Brien, *The Essential Plotinus,* p. 84.

12

Conclusion

Let us return to John Burnet's summary of the nature of Greek philosophy, which was quoted in the first chapter:

> Greek philosophy . . . is dominated from beginning to end by the problem of reality [meaning metaphysical reality]. In the last resort the question is always: "What is real?". . .
>
> The problem of reality, in fact, involves the problem of man's relation to it, which at once takes us beyond pure science. We have to ask whether the mind of man can have any contact with reality at all, and if it can, what difference this will make to his life. To anyone who has tried to live in sympathy with the Greek philosophers, the suggestion that they were "intellectualists" must seem ludicrous. On the contrary, Greek philosophy is based on the faith that reality is divine, and that the one thing needful is for the soul, which is akin to the divine, to enter into communion with it. It was in truth an effort to satisfy what we call the religious instinct. Ancient religion was a somewhat external thing, and made little appeal to this except in the "mysteries," and even the mysteries were apt to become external, and were peculiarly liable to corruption. We shall see again and again that philosophy sought to do for men what the mysteries could only do in part, and that it therefore includes most of what we should now call religion.[169]

Putting that last sentence into modern psychological terminology, one could say that Greek philosophy includes most of what we now call the archetypal level of the collective unconscious, the religion-creating layer of the psyche.

The Greek philosophers expounded some of the major archetypal concepts concerning the nature of psychic reality. For the Milesians it was *physis* (nature) and *arche* (the primal, original matter). For Pythagoras it was *arithmos* (number) and the *tetractys* (the divine image of quarternity). For Heraclitus it was *enantia* (the opposites) and *enantiodromia* (the turning into the opposite). For Parmenides it was *aletheia* (truth) and *doxa* (opinion). For Anaxagoras it was *nous* (mind). For Empedocles it was *rhizomata* (the four roots), which were later called the four elements, and *katharsis* (purification). For Socrates it was *maieusis* (the art of obstetrics). For Plato it was *eidos* (the eternal form or idea) and *anamnesis* (recollection of what was forgotten at birth). For Aristotle it was *aition* (the four causes) and *entelecheia* (a term which means both potential at

---

[169] *Greek Philosophy*, pp. 11f.

the beginning and realization at the end.) For Zeno of Citium it was *logos*. For Philo it was *allegoria*. For Plotinus it was the three hypostases of being: *hen, nous* and *psyche* (the One, the mind and the soul).

The phenomenon of Greek philosophy lasted about 1,000 years. It is conventionally said to have begun with the flourishing date of Thales: 585 B.C. It ends at 529 A.D. with the closing of the last school of philosophy in Athens, when the Roman Emperor, the Christian Justinian, forbade the teaching of philosophy.

The nineteenth-century historian Eduard Zeller summed up Greek philosophy as follows:

> Boldly, almost impetuously, Greek philosophy had in the 6th century B.C. trod the way which leads from myth to the Logos. Trusting in the power of the human mind, the great pre-Socratic Ionians, Plato and Aristotle built up their systems on a basis of science and superseded the mythical ideas. . . . But at an early date this rationalistic tendency was crossed by a religious influence, which originated . . . in the East. This was Orphicism, which with its separation of body and soul, matter and mind, god and the world grafted dualism upon Greek thought and relied upon divine revelations instead of rational proof. The Greek mind in men like Pythagoras . . . Empedocles and Plato endeavored to comprehend this doctrine and elaborate it on rational grounds. But it remained something foreign in Greek intellectual life. . . . [Then] the power of philosophical speculation which had been weakened by skepticism showed itself in neo-Pythagoreanism [a later development and also in] the Hellenistic-Jewish philosophy and in neo-Platonism as no longer strong enough to dam the stream of religious mysticism which was now sweeping in full force into philosophy. However much we may admire the last revival of antique thought in the philosophic system of Plotinus, it nevertheless bears the stamp of a non-Greek nature and traces of decadence which become more numerous and more pronounced in his successors. . . . Here knowledge is replaced by revelation in ecstasy. After Greek philosophy had performed this self-castration, it sank exhausted into the arms of religion; as Proclus [one of the neo-Platonist followers of Plotinus] expresses it in one of his hymns to the gods, "And so let me anchor, weary one, in the haven of piety."[170]

Zeller's position is one-sidedly rationalistic, supporting Greek rationalism against Eastern mysticism. That dualism, as Zeller calls it, can be understood psychologically as the tension between the two centers of the psyche, the ego and the Self. The fact is that in the course of psychological development, sooner or later, the ego must always sink exhausted into the arms of a religious attitude that acknowledges the supreme authority of the Self. The ego-centered, rationalistic person experiences it as a defeat, which is unavoidable so long as one is

---

[170] *Outlines of the History of Greek Philosophy,* pp. 336f.

unaware of the second center of the personality, the Self.

The legacy of Greek philosophy continued in various currents of the Western psyche. In the first two centuries of our era a profound eruption took place in the collective unconscious. It appeared first as a Jewish heresy centered around the figure of Christ, which then spread throughout the ancient world. It was a religion of salvation that appealed particularly to individuals who felt in need of deliverance, especially the vast slave population. It also had universal attraction because the psychological dominants of antiquity had decayed to such an extent that there was general despair just below the surface.

This new religion, which was a Jewish heresy and can therefore best be called a Jewish Christianity, encountered Greek philosophy, especially in Alexandria, and so gave rise to Gnosticism. Adolf Harnack defined Gnosticism as the acute Hellenizing of Christianity.[171] That same encounter, taking place gradually and more systematically, generated the theology of Catholic Christianity, which Harnack spoke of as the chronic Hellenizing of Christianity. In addition to Catholicism, other strains within Christian theology were mysticism, which took over much of Plotinus, and later medieval philosophy, which borrowed substantially from Aristotle. In the other major tradition, Greek philosophy encountered Egyptian technology, artisanship and embalming to generate alchemy.

There were three main pathways by which Greek philosophy survived and made its way into the modern psyche: the pathway that led to Catholic Christian theology, the one that led to alchemy, and a third pathway in which Greek philosophy went underground and then resurfaced in the Renaissance, about 1450, as Humanism. This is where the modern ego was born.

Through the previous chapters, it has been apparent that as Greek philosophy evolved it changed from an initial preoccupation with *physis* or nature to a preoccupation with the spiritual realm beyond nature. This development reached its peak in Plotinus. When Christianity encountered Greek philosophy it embraced its spiritual aspects and demonized the Greeks' worship of nature. Dionysus and Pan, the God of nature, were turned into the Devil.

It was this divine aspect of nature that was lost in Christianity and resurfaced in alchemy and the Renaissance. As it reappeared in the fourteenth and fifteenth centuries, prospects of ego development came with it. It brought a reevaluation of nature, matter, the relation to the sensible world—and those issues pertaining to the ego. It was centered in Florence, where Renaissance scholars began avidly

---

[171] *The History of Dogma,* vol. 1, p. 227.

collecting lost manuscripts of antiquity, often preserved unread in monastery libraries. These were translated into Latin and modern languages. The fall of Constantinople to the Turks in 1453 marked the loss of the eastern Roman empire to Christendom, and was a further impetus, as the treasures of the empire were sent back to Italy. Under the auspices of the Medici, many lost Greek manuscripts were translated. The new movement was named Humanism.

Two outstanding personalities marked the beginning of Humanism: Marsilio Ficino (1433-1499) and Giovanni Pico della Mirandola (1463-1494). The philosopher Will Durant summarizes the importance of these figures:

> [Ficino devoted] almost all his life to translating Plato into Latin and to studying, teaching and writing about Platonism. In youth he was so handsome the maidens of Florence eyed him possessively, but he cared less for them than for his books. For a time he lost his religious faith; Platonism seemed superior; he addressed his students as "beloved in Plato" rather than "beloved in Christ;" he burned candles before a bust of Plato, and adored him as a saint. Christianity appeared to him, in this mood, as but one of the many religions that hid elements of truth behind their allegorical dogmas and symbolic rites.
>
> . . . Count Giovanni Pico della Mirandola [was] the most fascinating personality in the Platonic Academy. . . . [He made] Florence his home. His eager mind took up one study after another—poetry, philosophy, architecture, music—and achieved in each some outstanding excellence. . . . [He was] a paragon in whom Nature had united all her gifts: "tall and finely molded, with something of divinity shining in his face"; a man of penetrating glance, indefatigable study, miraculous memory, and ecumenical erudition, eloquent in several languages, a favorite with women and philosophers, and as lovable in character as he was handsome in person. . . . His mind was open to every philosophy and every faith; he could not find it in him to reject any system, any man.[172]

What makes these two Humanists so important is that they display the beginning of modern man's hubris. The work that Pico is most remembered for is a rather brief essay entitled, "Oration on the Dignity of Man." Russell Kirk, in his introduction to a translation of this work, comments:

> [The] "dignity of Man" is the manifesto of humanism. . . . [This] "is the primary meaning of the Renaissance: the rebirth of man in the likeness of God." The man of the Middle Ages was humble, conscious almost always of his fallen and sinful nature, feeling himself a miserable foul creature watched by an angry God. Through Pride fell the angels. But Pico and his brother humanists declared that man was only a little lower than the angels, a being capable of descending to unclean depths, indeed, but also having it within his power to become godlike. How

---

[172] *The Renaissance,* pp. 120f.

marvelous and splendid a creature is man! This is the theme of Pico's oration, elaborated with all the pomp and confidence that characterized the rising Humanist teachers. "In this idea . . . there lay a colossal *hybris* unknown to the Middle Ages, but also a tremendous spiritual impulse such as only modern times can show."[173]

This is the moment in the cultural history of the West when the God-image fell into the human psyche. It is significant that Doctor John Faustus, the historical figure behind the Faust legend, is said to have lived contemporaneously with Pico. His dates are supposed to have been 1480 to 1540. The content of Greek philosophy poured into the modern psyche, with a different effect than it had on the ancients. Then, it had generated a reverent attitude, but some ego development had occurred since then, and it was as though the inflated stage of ego development now supervened.

The second pathway by which Greek philosophy was incorporated in the modern psyche was by its assimilation into Catholic theology and medieval thought. This is a huge subject in itself, but one particular issue has special psychological import. There was a great argument in medieval thought concerning the nature of what were called the universals. This was the medieval term that corresponded to Plato's "ideas." The question was, are the universals real or are they just names, *nomina?*

Those who said they were real were called the realists, and the ones who said they were just names, just abstractions and had no substantial meaning on their own, were called the nominalists. Jung discusses this opposition between the realists and the nominalists and considers that the division represents the difference between introverts and extraverts. For the nominalists, the universals exist only in their manifestation in things, so that the formula that they used was that the being, the *esse* of the universals, is in the thing: *esse in re*. But for the realists, the universals have a real existence corresponding to the realm of the *nous* of the Greeks, an existence in the intellect. Their formula was: *esse in intellectu.* Jung proposes to solve that conflict, as Jungian psychology can so often do with its understanding of the opposites, by the discovery of the third reconciling thing. In this case, he says that the third thing could be *esse in anima,* in other words, being in the psyche. He writes:

> *Esse in intellectu* lacks tangible reality, *esse in re* lacks mind. Idea and thing come together, however, in the human psyche, which holds the balance between them. What would the idea amount to if the psyche did not provide its living value? What would the thing be worth if the psyche withheld from it the determining

---

[173] "Oration," in Pico della Mirandola, *Oration on the Dignity of Man.*pp. xiiif.

force of the sense-impression? What indeed is reality if it is not a reality in ourselves, an *esse in anima?* Living reality is the product neither of the actual, objective behaviour of things nor of the formulated idea exclusively, but rather of the combination of both in the living psychological process, through *esse in anima.* Only through the specific vital activity of the psyche does the sense-impression attain that intensity, and the idea that effective force, which are the two indispensable constituents of living reality.

This autonomous activity of the psyche . . . is, like every vital process, a continually creative act. The psyche creates reality every day. The only expression I can use for this activity is *fantasy.*[174]

The third stream in which Greek philosophy left a major deposit is the stream of alchemy. It was noted earlier that Greek philosophy, at least in its later development, became very largely an agent of *sublimatio,* of a spiritualization that tended to depreciate matter and the body and nature, and therefore, by those depreciations, implicitly depreciated the ego, which is symbolized by those images of body and matter. A very interesting thing happened then, just when Neo-Platonism was coming into full flower. In Alexandria—where, as Jung's "Seven Sermons to the Dead" puts it, "East meets West"—Greek philosophy encountered Egyptian technology, artisanship and embalming procedures. It became attached to very concrete practical techniques of manipulating matter, such banal and dubious activities as coating base metal to make it look like gold and selling it fraudulently as gold. It was not all that suspect, but it could stoop that low. The processes of dyeing and metallurgy, and the preoccupation with the refining of valuable metals, were all part of Egyptian technology.

So the abstract ideas that in earlier centuries had had a living relation to their material origin, but had since been sublimated so that they became intellectual abstractions, now joined with these various technical procedures. As a result, they were reconnected with the earth. The result was that Greek philosophy became a laboratory operation—unheard of from the standpoint of the Greek philosophers—but that is what happened as alchemy developed.

There is a medieval alchemical picture showing the alchemist's chamber having two rooms.[175] One room is a laboratory, a hot and grimy place where a furnace is being stoked by the laboratory assistant. The other room is a library, where someone calmly consults books. Those are the two sides, Egyptian technology and the library, joined in the alchemical process. This picture applies

---

[174] *Psychological Types,* CW 6, pars. 77f.

[175] See *Psychology and Alchemy,* CW 12, fig. 144.

specifically to the opus of individuation, which has two aspects. On the one hand, it is an operation involving imagery and abstract ideas, and at the same time, it is a process of concrete living experience in which the imagery that emerges is applied—in the laboratory of life, so to speak. We can say that in the process of individuation, the individual ego is the laboratory for the creation of consciousness.

Jung has some profound remarks to make about the way alchemy developed in the collective psyche. They are found in *Psychology and Alchemy:*

> Alchemy is rather like an undercurrent to the Christianity that ruled on the surface . . . the primordial matriarchal world . . . was overthrown by the masculine world of the father. The historical shift in the world's consciousness towards the masculine [was] compensated by the . . . unconscious. In certain pre-Christian religions the differentiation of the masculine principle had taken the form of the father-son specification, a change which was to be of utmost importance for Christianity.[176]

Here, in the phrase "the father-son specification," Jung refers to the fact that the Christian dogma of the Trinity had established the image of Christ as the son of the supreme Deity, the father. That is the "father-son specification," and that illustrates how the masculine world overthrew the primordial matriarchal world. That is why the Christian Trinity is all male. He continues:

> Were the unconscious merely complementary, this shift of consciousness would have been accompanied by the production of a mother and daughter, for which the necessary material lay ready to hand in the myth of Demeter and Persephone. But, as alchemy shows, the unconscious chose rather the Cybele-Attis type in the form of the *prima materia* and the *filius macrocosmi,* thus proving that it is not complementary but compensatory.[177]

Here, Jung is referring to the fact that the alchemical theological fantasy was that out of the matriarchal *prima materia* the Philosophers' Stone would be born, one of whose names was the son of the macrocosm, *filius macrocosmi,* "son of the great world." Jung is pointing out that the collective unconscious in the Middle Ages, instead of compensating the one-sided masculine Trinity of father and son by creating a mother and daughter, created instead a mother and son, a maternal *prima materia* giving birth to the son of the macrocosm.

> This goes to show that the unconscious does not simply act *contrary* to the conscious mind but *modifies* it more in the manner of an opponent or partner. The son

---

[176] Ibid., par. 26.
[177] Ibid.

type does not call up a daughter as a complementary image from the depths of the "chthonic" unconscious—it calls up another son. This remarkable fact would seem to be connected with the incarnation in our earthly human nature of a purely spiritual God, brought about by the Holy Ghost impregnating the womb of the Blessed Virgin. Thus the higher, the spiritual, the masculine inclines to the lower, the earthly, the feminine; and accordingly, the mother, who was anterior to the world of the father, accommodates herself to the masculine principle and, with the aid of the human spirit (alchemy or "the philosophy"), produces a son—not the antithesis of Christ but rather his chthonic counterpart, not a divine man but a fabulous being conforming to the nature of the primordial mother.[178]

In other words, the myth of the birth of Christ, which takes place by the impregnation of the ordinary woman Mary by the Holy Spirit, indicates that the masculine spiritual principle has an inclination to—"inclines"—to the feminine. Thus, the masculine principle does not haughtily remain aloof from the matriarchal feminine, but bends down to her and allows himself to be regenerated as a son in her womb. In response to that gesture of generosity, the matriarchal principle replies in kind and does not insist on generating a daughter, but meets the masculine principle halfway by generating a son. Those unfamiliar with the psychological applications may think this is abstruse abstraction that does not matter much, but it is quite the contrary. It refers to the nature of the ego's relation to the unconscious, and when an individual starts to deal with the dynamic represented by these images, it is of the greatest importance that the unconscious is willing to meet the ego halfway. Jung goes on:

And just as the redemption of man the microcosm is the task of the "upper" son, so the "lower" son has the function of a *salvator macrocosmi* [savior of the world].[179]

According to the Christian salvation myth, the world is not redeemed; human beings who cling to Christ are saved, but not the world itself. The world is still in for some disaster, according to the Christian mythology. But according to alchemical mythology, if the Philosophers' Stone comes into being, it functions as a savior of the world. Since it comes out of matter, it reconciles the conflict between spirit and matter that had been previously generated by the father-son myth. Jung goes on:

This, in brief, is the drama that was played out in the obscurities of alchemy. It is superfluous to remark that these two sons were never united, except perhaps in the mind and innermost experience of a few particularly gifted alchemists. But it is not

[178] Ibid.
[179] Ibid.

very difficult to see the "purpose" of this drama: in the Incarnation [of Christ] it looked as though the masculine principle of the father-world were approximating to the feminine principle of the mother-world, with the result that the latter felt impelled to approximate in turn to the father-world. What it evidently amounted to was an attempt to bridge the gulf separating the two worlds as compensation for the open conflict between them.[180]

The process described above displays all the characteristic features of psychological compensation. We know that the mask of the unconscious is not rigid—it reflects the face we turn towards it. Hostility lends it a threatening aspect, friendliness softens its features. It is not a question of mere optical reflection [the compensatory function of the unconscious], but of an autonomous answer which reveals the self-sufficing nature of that which answers. [We are answered by another personality.] Thus the *filius philosophorum* is not just the reflected image, in unsuitable material, of the son of God; on the contrary, this son of Tiamat reflects the features of the primordial maternal figure. Although he is decidedly hermaphroditic he has a masculine name—a sign that the chthonic underworld, having been rejected by the spirit and identified with evil, has a tendency to compromise. There is no mistaking the fact that he is a concession to the spiritual and masculine principle, even though he carries in himself the weight of the earth and the whole fabulous nature of primordial animality.

   This answer of the mother-world shows that the gulf between it and the father-world is not unbridgeable, seeing that the unconscious holds the seed of the unity of both.[181]

To conclude, these three streams have been considered: Renaissance Humanism; the theology of the Christian Church together with its modifications by the Protestant reformers; and the stream of alchemy, which, together with the rational investigative spirit that was generated by the Renaissance, gave birth to science as we know it. These streams are the major sources of the modern Western psyche. Jung has said that the modern mind has two parents: its mother is the Church and its father is science. Behind these parents are other quite important ancestors, among whom are the ancient Greek philosophers.

---

[180] Ibid., par. 27.

[181] Ibid., pars. 29f.

Publisher's Tribute to Edward F. Edinger

The world is full of unconscious people—those who don't know why they do what they do. Edward Edinger did as much as anyone I know to correct this situation. To my mind, he was as true to Jung as one can be. Like Marie-Louise von Franz, he was a classic Jungian, pure and simple, by which I mean he took Jung's message to heart and amplified it according to his own talents. In a review of von Franz's *C.G. Jung: His Myth in Our Time,* he described her as "a true spiritual daughter of Jung, a carrier of the pure Jungian elixir." Well, Dr. Edinger was a true spiritual son of Jung.

For those who find Jung himself tough going, Edinger has been the pre-eminent interpreter for more than thirty years. In lectures, books, tapes and videos, he has masterfully presented the distilled essence of Jung's work, illuminating its relevance to both collective and individual psychology. Thus his *Mysterium Lectures,* for instance, is not only a brilliant scholarly study of Jung's *Mysterium Coniunctionis* and arcane alchemical operations, it is also a practical guide to what is going on in the laboratory of the unconscious.

After Inner City published his book *The Creation of Consciousness* in 1984, we enjoyed a warm working relationship. I visited him a couple of times at his home in Los Angeles, and sent him copies of each new Inner City title as it was published. He always responded quickly with a hand-written letter giving his considered opinion. Of course, not everything we published was his cup of tea, but he respected my choice of manuscripts—and the books I wrote myself—as deriving from my own process of individuation: where my energy, at that time, wanted to go.

Every year or two Dr. Edinger offered Inner City Books a new manuscript. We took them all because they were good meaty stuff. Clean, crisp writing, no padding, no nonsense, no blather. Never mind that they would not appear on the New York Times list of best-sellers; they fit perfectly with our self-professed mandate "to promote the understanding and practical application" of Jung's work. More than that, their content has kept me psychologically alert.

We are proud to now have twelve Edinger titles under our wing, including this two-volume set, *The Psyche in Antiquity.* Thanks to the devoted energy of others and the co-operation of his wife, Dianne D. Cordic, more Edinger will be available in the future. Watch for these gems: 1) *The Psyche on Stage: Individuation Motifs in Shakespeare and Sophocles;* 2) *The Old Testament Prophets: The Bible and the Psyche, Book 2;* and 3) *The Sacred Psyche: A Psychological Approach to the Psalms.*

Personally, I loved the man. I feel privileged and fortunate indeed to be in a position to keep his work and spirit alive, to the benefit of all those who strive to be conscious.

Daryl Sharp

119

Bibliography

Aquinas, Thomas. *Basic Writings of St. Thomas Aquinas.* Ed. Anton C. Pegis. New York: Random House, 1945.

Armstrong, A.H., trans. and ed. *Plotinus.* London: George Allen and Unwin Ltd., 1913.

Arnold, Matthew. *Poetry and Criticism of Matthew Arnold.* Ed. A. Dwight Culler. New York: Houghton-Mifflin, 1961.

Bambrough, Renford. *The Philosophy of Aristotle.* New York: Mentor Books, 1963.

Barnes, Jonathan. *Early Greek Philosophy.* London: Penguin Books, 1987.

Bevan, Edwyn. *Stoics and Sceptics.* Oxford: Clarendon Press, 1913.

Burkert, Walter. *Lore and Science in Ancient Pythagoreanism.* Trans. Edwin L. Minar, Jr. Cambridge, MA: Harvard University Press, 1972.

Burnet, John. *Early Greek Philosophy.* New York: World Publishing Co., 1962.

_____. *Greek Philosophy: Thales to Plato.* New York: Meridian Books, 1960.

Cornford, F.M. *From Religion to Philosophy.* New York: Harper and Brothers, 1957.

Diogenes Laertius. *Lives of the Eminent Philosophers.* Ed. and Trans. R.D. Hicks. Loeb Classical Library. Cambridge, MA: Harvard University Press, 1959.

Durant, Will. *The Renaissance.* New York: Simon and Schuster, 1953.

Edinger, Edward F. *Anatomy of the Psyche: Alchemical Symbolism in Psychotherapy.* La Salle, Il: Open Court, 1985.

_____. *Ego and Archetype: Individuation and the Religious Function of the Psyche.* Boston: Shambhala Publications, 1992.

_____. *The Mysterium Lectures: A Journey through Jung's* Mysterium Coniunctionis. Toronto: Inner City Books, 1995.

Emerson, Ralph Waldo. *Selected Writings of Ralph Waldo Emerson.* Ed. Brooks Atkinson. New York: Modern Library, Random House, 1950.

Fowler, H.N., trans. *Plato.* Cambridge, MA: Harvard University Press, Loeb Classical Library, 1962.

Glatzer, Nahum N., ed. *The Essential Philo.* New York: Schocken Books, 1971.

Goethe, Johann Wolfgang. *Faust.* Trans. Barker Fairley. Toronto: University of Toronto Press, 1985.

Goodenough, Erwin R. *An Introduction to Philo Judeaus.* Oxford: Basil Blackwell, 1962.

Guirdham, Arthur. *The Cathars and Reincarnation.* Wheaton, Il: Theosophical Publishing House, 1978.

Hamilton, Edith, and Cairns, Huntington, eds. *Plato's Collected Dialogues.* Trans. F.M. Cornford. New York: Bollingen Foundation, 1961.

Hatch, Edwin. *The Influence of Greek Ideas and Usages Upon the Christian Church.* London: Williams and Norgate, 1891.

Hicks, R.D. trans. and ed. *Lives of the Eminent Philosophers.* Loeb Classical Library. Cambridge, MA: Harvard University Press, 1959.

_____. *Stoic and Epicurean.* New York: Russell, 1962.

Hölderlin, Friedrich. *Poems and Fragments.* Trans. Michael Hamburger. Ann Arbor, MI: University of Michigan Press, 1967.

Jowett, B., trans. *The Dialogues of Plato.* New York: Random House, 1937.

Jung, C.G. *C.G. Jung Speaking.* Ed. William McGuire and R.F.C. Hull. Princeton.: Princeton University Press, 1977.

_____. *The Collected Works* (Bollingen Series XX). 20 vols. Trans. R.F.C. Hull. Ed. H. Read, M. Fordham, G. Adler, Wm. McGuire. Princeton: Princeton University Press, 1953-1979.

_____. *Letters* (Bollingen Series XCV). 2 vols. Trans. R.F.C. Hull. Ed. Gerhard Adler and Aniela Jaffé. Princeton: Princeton University Press, 1975.

_____. *Memories, Dreams, Reflections.* Ed. Aniela Jaffé. New York: Random House, 1963.

_____. *Nietzsche's Zarathustra* (Bollingen Series XCIX). 2 vols. Ed. J.L. Jarrett. Princeton: Princeton University Press, 1988.

Kirk, G.S., and Raven, J.E. *The Presocratic Philosophers.* Cambridge, MA: Cambridge University Press, 1957.

MacKenna, Stephen, trans. *Plotinus: The Enneads.* London: Faber and Faber, 1962.

Nagy, Marilyn. *Philosophical Issues in the Psychology of C.G. Jung.* Albany, NY: State University of New York Press, 1991.

Neumann, Erich. *The Origins and History of Consciousness* (Bollingen Series XLII). Princeton: Princeton University Press, 1969.

New International Dictionary of New Testament Theology. Grand Rapids, MI: Zondervan Publishing House, 1975-1978.

Nietzsche, Friederich. *Basic Writings of Nietzsche.* Trans. and ed. Walter Kaufmann. New York: Random House (Modern Library), 1968.

_____. *Beyond Good and Evil.* New York: Random House, 1966.

_____. *My Sister and I.* New York: Bridgehead Books, 1954.

_____. *Philosophy in the Tragic Age of the Greeks.* Washington, DC: Henry Regnery Co., Gateway Edition, 1962.

O'Brien, Elmer, ed. *The Essential Plotinus.* Indianapolis: Hackett Publishing Co., 1964.

Peters, F.E. *Greek Philosophical Terms: A Historical Lexicon.* New York: New York University Press, 1967.

Pico della Mirandola, Giovanni. *Oration on the Dignity of Man.* Trans. A.P. Caponigri. South Bend, IN.: Regnery/Gateway Inc., 1956.

Roberts, Alexander .J., and Donaldson, James, eds. *The Ante-Nicene Fathers.* Grand Rapids, MI: Wm. B. Eerdmans Publishng Co., 1986.

Rohde, Erwin. *Psyche: The Cult of Souls in Ancient Greece.* New York: Harcourt, Brace and Co., 1925.

Runes, Dagobert D., ed. *Dictionary of Philosophy.* New York: Philosophical Lib., 1960.

Snell, Bruno. *The Discovery of Mind.* Cambridge, MA: Harvard University Press, 1953.

von Franz, Marie-Louise. *Dreams.* Boston: Shambhala Publications, 1991.

_____. *Number and Time.* Evanston, IL: Northwestern University Press, 1974.

Wordsworth, William. *Poetical Works.* London: Oxford University Press, 1969.

Zeller, Eduard. *Outlines of the History of Greek Philosophy.* New York: Meridian Books, 1931.

Index

Also by Edward F. Edinger

THE AION LECTURES
Exploring the Self in Jung's *Aion*
ISBN 0-919123-72-4. (1996) 208 pp. 30 illustrations *Sewn* $18

MELVILLE'S MOBY-DICK: An American Nekyia
ISBN 0-919123-70-8. (1995) 160 pp. *Sewn* $16

THE MYSTERIUM LECTURES
A Journey Through Jung's *Mysterium Coniunctionis*
ISBN 0-919123-66-X. (1995) 352 pp. 90 illustrations *Sewn* $20

THE MYSTERY OF THE CONIUNCTIO
Alchemical Image of Individuation
ISBN 0-919123-67-8. (1994) 112 pp. 48 illustrations *Sewn* $14

TRANSFORMATION OF THE GOD-IMAGE
An Elucidation of Jung's *Answer to Job*
ISBN 0-919123-55-4. (1992) 144 pp. *Sewn* $16

GOETHE'S FAUST: Notes for a Jungian Commentary
ISBN 0-919123-44-9. (1990) 112 pp. *Sewn* $15

THE CHRISTIAN ARCHETYPE
A Jungian Commentary on the Life of Christ
ISBN 0-919123-27-9. (1987) 144 pp. 34 illustrations *Sewn* $16

THE BIBLE AND THE PSYCHE
Individuation Symbolism in the Old Testament
ISBN 0-919123-23-6. (1986) 176 pp. *Sewn* $18

ENCOUNTER WITH THE SELF: A Jungian Commentary on
William Blake's *Illustrations of the Book of Job*
ISBN 0-919123-21-X. (1986) 80 pp. 22 illustrations *Sewn* $12

THE CREATION OF CONSCIOUSNESS
Jung's Myth for Modern Man
ISBN 0-919123-13-9. (1984) 128 pp. 10 illustrations *Sewn* $15